A Practical Guide to Examinership

Neil Hughes, FCA

with

Dessie Morrow

Conor Noone

Sarah-Jane O'Keeffe

Diarmaid Guthrie

Anna Sadon

CHARTERED
ACCOUNTANTS
IRELAND

Published in 2021 by
Chartered Accountants Ireland
Chartered Accountants House, 47 Pearse Street, Dublin 2
The Linenhall, 32-38 Linenhall Street, Belfast BT2 8BG
www.charteredaccountants.ie

ISBN: 978-1-908199-37-9

Typeset by Datapage
Printed and bound by CPI Group (UK) Ltd, Croydon, CR0 4YY

Contents

Foreword

by Mr Justice Michael Quinn

This guide is a welcome publication which will serve as a valuable tool both for specialist professional practitioners and for any reader interested in the practical dimensions of examinership.

The author has a vast knowledge of the subject and shares his experiences ranging from complex high-value cases through to interesting examples of how the process, properly utilised in appropriate cases, can serve small and medium enterprises and local communities.

The guide contains an interesting insight into the evolution of examinership from its introduction in 1990. The author puts the important changes made in 1999 in their context as responses to shortcomings in the process which were identified in its early years, particularly the challenge of striking the balance between the interests of competing stakeholders.

The author is a strong advocate for the process. Nonetheless, the guide describes very frankly the advantages and disadvantages of examinership. There are useful chapters identifying particular difficulties for the process, most notably the challenge of making the process a success in a cost proportionate manner for small and medium enterprises. He brings together a compendium highlighting which types of company are truly suitable for examinership, by contrast with those that have been shown to be unsuitable.

The author puts examinership in its context by reference to the EU Directive on Preventive Restructuring and Insolvency and Discharge Procedures, which Member States are required to implement by 17 July 2021. Albeit that the timing of the passing of the 1990 Act was prompted by the immediate needs presented by the *Goodman* case, he observes on the prescience of the Irish legislature by introducing 30 years ago concepts that are only now to become standard throughout the EU.

Any reader who faces the experience of an examinership, either as a stakeholder, advisor or commentator, will find the guide easily readable, and free of jargon and excessively technical language. Although not a legal textbook, the author has cited vast numbers of reported cases spanning the period from the inception of examinership, through different cycles in the economy, through to the latest challenges of the pandemic and Brexit. The appendices include case studies and a copy of Statement of Insolvency Practice 19B, and are a useful addition and easy point of reference for readers.

Restructuring solutions will always be at the heart of business change. Examinership will never be the only remedy or alternative to liquidation or receivership, but it has proved to be a success. The experience developed by our practitioners and courts has also shown that this process can place Ireland among the leaders in cross-border restructurings and an attractive and effective forum for complex cases. This guide will serve as a valuable resource to support the promotion of this process.

I commend the guide and congratulate the author and Chartered Accountants Ireland on its publication.

Michael Quinn
The High Court
Dublin 7
25 January 2021

Contributors

Dessie Morrow, ACA, is Director at Baker Tilly and has worked with its Corporate Recovery team since 2006. He has extensive examinership experience from over 150 cases. Dessie is a registered insolvency practitioner and appointment-taker, and has acted as an examiner, receiver, official liquidator, creditors' voluntary liquidator and members' voluntary liquidator.

Conor Noone, ACA, is Senior Manager at Baker Tilly, working with its Corporate Recovery department since 2010. He has extensive experience of corporate finance/sale of business transactions, creditors' voluntary liquidations, court liquidations, receiverships and examinerships, as well as business review and turnaround. Conor is a registered insolvency practitioner and appointment-taker, and has acted as an examiner, official liquidator and members' voluntary liquidator.

Sarah-Jane O'Keeffe, ACCA, is Senior Manager at Baker Tilly and a member of its Corporate Governance team. She was Ireland's first-appointed female examiner. In 2018, Sarah-Jane was shortlisted in the Accountant of the Year category of the Irish Early Career Awards. She has a career working in practice since 2009, both for accountancy and legal firms, and has extensive experience in advising and examining companies from a statutory and commercial perspective.

Diarmaid Guthrie, ACA, is Senior Manager in the Corporate Recovery department at Baker Tilly, where he leads one of the department's teams, assisting companies and individuals in turning around their businesses since 2013. His experience includes forensic accounting and investigations, as well as business restructuring and advisory, primarily in examinership and receivership cases. Diarmaid has also worked on secondment at Baker Tilly's office in Nicosia, Cyprus, where he provided advisory services to a major Cypriot bank on their non-performing loan book.

Anna Sadon, FCCA, works in the Corporate Recovery department at Baker Tilly as part of the senior management team. She has been working in restructuring since 2002 and has extensive knowledge of examinerships and receiverships, as well as liquidations of solvent and insolvent companies. Anna also has experience of compliance and risk management at both departmental and firm level.

Acknowledgements

I would like to extend my sincere thanks to the past and current members of the Baker Tilly restructuring teams in both Dublin and Nicosia, who worked on the many cases that form the basis of this book. Without all of their efforts over the years, we would not have had the opportunity to build up the direct experience of examinership that we have drawn upon in writing this text.

This book would have been impossible without the expertise and hard work of the contributors who wrote the bulk of the text in many of the chapters. My sincere thanks to Dessie Morrow, Conor Noone, Sarah-Jane O'Keeffe, Diarmaid Guthrie and Anna Sadon; and also to their colleagues Eoin Healy and particularly Faye Quinn for proof-reading the text and for working with our friends in Chartered Accountants Ireland to drive the final drafts to a conclusion.

This is my second opportunity to work with Michael Diviney of Chartered Accountants Ireland. His expertise as editor was hugely important to us in ensuring that the text flowed and stayed true to our original goal of writing an accessible practical guide rather than a legal textbook. Examinership is a legal process, however, and I would also like to acknowledge our friends and colleagues in the legal profession, too many to mention, whose advice and intuition have proven absolutely invaluable to the success of cases throughout the years. I would also especially like to express my sincere appreciation to Mr Justice Michael Quinn for his detailed foreword.

Finally, and most importantly, I and all of the contributors would like to express our deepest gratitude to our families for the support they have given us in the time taken to write this book.

Table of Cases

1.

Introduction

- What is Examinership?
- The Term 'Examinership'
- Key Features of Examinership
- The Underuse of Examinership
- Examinership in an International Context
- About this Guide

What is Examinership?

Examinership is a legal process available in the Republic of Ireland (and also in the Republic of Cyprus) to rescue companies from insolvency. As stated by Des O'Malley TD, Minister for Industry and Commerce, in 1990 as the Dáil debated the introduction of legislation underpinning examinership:

> "To use a medical analogy, these provisions are intended to be of use to companies that are temporarily 'sick' — I would not normally expect to see them being used by healthy companies or indeed in the final analysis by companies that are terminally ill.

> The central feature of what is being proposed is the appointment to a company by the High Court of an expert, called an examiner in the Bill, and the placing of the company concerned under the protection of the Court for a limited period."[1]

Insolvency is a normal part of commerce. Business failure is a fact of life in any economy and for a wide variety of reasons, for example:

- a company may have suffered large bad debts or trading losses in poor economic conditions, or did not cut costs swiftly enough following a downturn;
- there may simply have been insufficient demand for a company's products or services for the undertaking to be viable (the failure of practically all of the major Irish property development companies in the period 2008 to 2011 and the difficulties faced by Cypriot property development companies in the period since 2013 are cases in point).

Insolvency will often result in a liquidation of the company, which will usually mean the doors being closed and staff being made redundant. Where there is a secured creditor in place, a receivership process may be another option.

While it is true that some businesses are rendered terminally insolvent, with no hope of recovery, regardless of what restructuring, investment or business remodelling techniques are brought to bear, many businesses that find themselves insolvent *are* capable of survival if they undergo fundamental restructuring. Typically, the result of such a restructuring will be better than liquidation for all stakeholders of the company, with benefits for the business owner, employees, creditors, the state and wider society.

---

[1] Extract from the Dáil Éireann debate, Second Stage, Companies (Amendment) Bill 1990, 28 August 1990, Vol. 401 No. 8.

The Term 'Examinership'

The process now known as 'examinership' was originally introduced in Ireland by the Companies (Amendment) Act 1990 and has since been extensively updated and modified. The process was introduced in Cyprus in 2015 at the insistence of the European Commission, the European Central Bank and the IMF – colloquially called the 'European Troika' – as a result of the 2012–2013 Cypriot financial crisis. This new Cypriot insolvency framework was largely based on existing Irish legislation.

The term 'examinership' does not feature at all in any part of the legislation that introduced it, or indeed, in any amendments to that legislation; nor was it mentioned in the Irish parliamentary debates of August 1990 when the original Bill was rushed through both houses of the Oireachtas.[2] In fact, the official title of the business recovery process that is the subject of this book is 'examination'. Shortly after its introduction, professionals working in the area began to prefer the term 'examinership'.

Between 1990 and 1999 the process was increasingly referred to as 'examinership' rather than examination. The companies that availed of the new process had to describe themselves as being "under the protection of the Court", as required by section 12 of the Companies (Amendment) Act 1990. The use of the term 'examinership' was still retained even when the process was specifically described as 'examination' in section 20 of the Irish Companies (Amendment) (No. 2) Act 1999. This section contained a very specific requirement wherein every company under court protection had to ensure that "every invoice, order for goods or business letter issued by or on behalf of the company, being a document on or in which the name of the company appears, shall, immediately after the mention of that name, include the words 'in examination (under the Companies (Amendment) Act, 1990)'." Nevertheless, the procedure continues now to be universally known in practice as 'examinership' in both jurisdictions, in court and in public discourse, and this is the term predominantly used in this book.

Key Features of Examinership

The overarching intent of examinership is to save otherwise viable enterprises from closure, thereby saving the jobs of the employees whose livelihoods depend on them. An examinership is administered

---

[2] The Irish parliament. It was recalled during the summer recess to prevent the imminent collapse of the Goodman Group of meat processing companies, as described in **Chapter 2**.

by a court-appointed examiner, who is invariably an accountant in practice with insolvency experience.

As referred to above, if the examinership process is not a viable option for a company, other forms of insolvency procedure will likely occur, such as a receivership instigated by a secured creditor or a creditors' voluntary liquidation. In a receivership, the role of the receiver is to 'receive' the assets of the company and realise them for the benefit of the charge-holder, which is usually the company's lender. A creditors' voluntary liquidation is a process whereby a liquidator is appointed to an insolvent company following a creditors' meeting. The liquidator will generally investigate the reason for insolvency and manage the assets and pay creditors in legal preference to ultimately dissolve the company.

In comparison to these insolvency procedures, when a company is placed into examination, the examiner considers the measures required to ensure that the company has a reasonable prospect of survival and formulates a proposal to the shareholders and creditors that has the effect of reducing the liabilities of the company by effectively compromising their claims as part of a rescue plan.

The Concept of 'Reasonable Prospect of Survival'

Examinership allows an insolvent company with a demonstrable 'reasonable prospect of survival' to apply for court protection from creditors who have outstanding claims, so that an examiner can devise a 'scheme of arrangement' (or compromise) to restore the company to solvency. Though there are numerous ways that such a scheme of arrangement can be facilitated by the examiner, invariably it will involve the payment of part of the company's debts over an agreed timeline. The usual method to fund the examiner's proposals is to secure some form of new investment or refinancing for the company.

The statutory requirement for a struggling company to have a 'reasonable prospect of survival' involves having to demonstrate with objective evidence that there exists a 'reasonable' chance of the company being rescued. The company needs to do this to be considered a viable examinership candidate (which is discussed further in Chapter 4).

The Provision of a Legal Framework

Regardless of the reasons for a company becoming insolvent, the examinership process provides a court-monitored process for the company to deal with all aspects of its insolvency, including, but not limited to, issues relating to creditors, employees, shareholders, directors, management, investors and onerous contracts (such as upwards-only property leases). Although other insolvency processes are set out in the Companies Act 2014, a marked difference of the examinership process is that it is court monitored for up to 100 days.

As mentioned above, an examinership is administered by a court-appointed examiner, who is given sufficient time to closely inspect the affairs of the business with a view to formulating the ultimate survival package by way of a scheme of arrangement with creditors. The authority of the court then renders the scheme legally binding on all shareholders and creditors of the company, even those who oppose the scheme of arrangement. Thus, examinership allows a company 'breathing space' from creditors to allow its trade to continue uninterrupted while the company is being turned around.

In certain unusual instances, the examiner will take over nominated executive functions, or the full running of the company, if this will facilitate its survival (as described more fully in Chapter 7). In practice this is very rare, and the existing directors remain in control of the business for the duration of the protection period. In fact, the High Court has consistently frowned on examiners exceeding their statutory functions and has on numerous occasions disallowed costs, deeming certain work carried out to have been unnecessary (see Chapter 11).

Job Protection

The principle of job protection has been articulated in many legal cases involving examinership, but perhaps most notably by Mr Justice Frank Clark (now Chief Justice), in the seminal *Traffic Group Limited* case, which involved the successful examinership of a fashion wholesaler in 2007:

> "It is clear that the principal focus of the legislation is to enable, in an appropriate case, an enterprise to continue in existence for the benefit of the economy as a whole and, of equal, or indeed greater, importance to enable as many as possible of the jobs which may be at stake in such enterprise to be maintained for the benefit of the community in which the relevant employment is located. It is important both for the court and, indeed, for examiners, to keep in mind that such is the focus of the legislation. It is not designed to help shareholders whose investment has proved to be unsuccessful. It is to seek to save enterprise and jobs."

As we shall see in Chapter 2, the importance of protecting employment has been re-iterated consistently both when the examinership process was introduced by statute and also by judges presiding over examinership cases during the subsequent evolution of the process. And the process has had considerable success in protecting employment. Our research has shown that more than 16,000 jobs were saved in Irish companies that successfully navigated the examinership process between 2010 and 2020. This does not include the jobs saved in numerous large companies; for example, approximately 5,000 jobs were saved in the *Eircom* examinership in 2012, the largest insolvency case in the EU that year. It is clear, therefore, that the process has had a considerable impact on the preservation of jobs in Ireland.

Critics of examinership as a corporate recovery option are quick to argue that some of the jobs saved by companies successfully coming through the process would have been preserved in any event, either by way of a new company purchasing the assets of the insolvent company in liquidation or by way of a trading receivership. However, many businesses do not re-emerge as a different corporate entity following liquidation or receivership; the business simply ceases to exist. Also, the above argument centres on the *roles* of employees rather than the actual people working for an insolvent company. It is cold comfort for a long-standing employee to know that their role will be preserved in a new company that will rise from the ashes of the old if that role is filled by a new staff member. In addition, the transfer of undertakings regulations as set out in the European Communities (Protection of Employees on Transfer of Undertakings) Regulations 2003 ('TUPE')[3] will not assist an employee in keeping their job if there is a cessation of trade.

The Underuse of Examinership

> *"It is a disappointment that it isn't used more widely because I think the mechanism is a useful one."*

> Des O'Malley, former Minister for Industry and Commerce

When one considers the low numbers of companies entering examinership each year, it is clear that the process remains relatively underused. For example, during the nadir of the Irish economic recession in 2011, there were 1,638 corporate insolvency and just 16 examinership cases (less than 0.1% of corporate insolvencies). There was an increase in 2012 to circa 0.15% when 27 examiners were appointed out of a total of 1,684 corporate insolvencies. At the time of writing, Irish companies continue to show a low propensity by international standards to enter into this

---

[3] S.I. No. 131 of 2003.

formal restructuring process (see below). In Cyprus, again at the time of writing, there has yet to be a successful examinership case, notwithstanding the introduction of the process there in 2015.

This can be compared to the numbers entering equivalent processes in the similar open-market economies of the United States and the United Kingdom, i.e. the so-called 'Chapter 11' process in the US and the process known as 'trading administration' in the UK. In 2018, the 5,962 business Chapter 11 petitions in the US amounted to 27% of all business cases filed that year. The 1,814 administrations carried out in the UK in 2019 represented 10.5% of all company insolvencies in that year. By comparison, examinership continues to be underused in Ireland and Cyprus, with only 1%–2% of insolvent companies per annum petitioning for court protection.

With the evidence confirming that golden opportunities to save critical jobs continue to be lost, the question arises: why do businesses not embrace the chance to restructure and survive through examinership? There are number of reasons:

1. Most of the years following the introduction of the legislation were marked by the huge economic growth of the 1990s, which then continued with relatively little interruption until the financial crisis of 2007–2008. During those years, there was simply no focus on formal corporate recovery measures as the majority of trading difficulties were addressed by fresh borrowing. For example, in an SME business with a financial hole in its bow, the principal would typically secure an inexpensive loan from a willing bank, the hole would be plugged and the business would continue.

2. Following the property crashes in Ireland in 2009 and Cyprus in 2013, there was a large number of high-profile, unsuccessful examinership petitions by owners of property development companies. In reality, those companies were inappropriate candidates for the examinership process in the first place, as they could not at that time meet the critical 'reasonable prospect of survival' criterion (see above). The cases in question were dismissed by the court as quasi asset-recovery exercises that did not meet with the job-saving purpose of the legislation. However, the failure of these property developer petitions (and the significant legal costs that followed) led to the examinership process being portrayed negatively in the media, which affected the views and mindset of company directors and their advisors. Consequently, petitioning rates for examinership remained low, even among fundamentally good companies likely to have been successful candidates for the process.

3. A lack of awareness of how the process works, and the skills required to advise clients about it, persists in the professional advisor community. This is a self-perpetuating problem: the less the process is used, the less professional advisors will feel comfortable in advising their clients to avail of it due to a lack of experience of the benefits it can bring to a struggling business. This contrasts with the routine practice in the US where accountants and lawyers regularly provide Chapter 11 advice. The practice of examinership in Ireland and Cyprus is concentrated in only a handful of professional accounting and legal firms, mostly based in the capital cities Dublin and Nicosia, which hinders more widespread adoption.

4. Between 1990 and 2012 in Ireland, the examinership process was exclusively administered in the High Court. Theoretically, during those years a company with liabilities of less than €317,434.52 could have sought to have its petition heard in a regional Circuit Court, but such applications were unheard of due to poor take-up of the process among smaller companies. For an SME business in a location far from Dublin (e.g. Donegal or Kerry), the thought of perhaps five visits to the High Court in Dublin to restructure their business was seen as impractical. In addition, the High Court carries with it an often-justified perception of high legal costs. The amended rules regarding Circuit Court examinership introduced in the Companies (Miscellaneous Provisions) Act 2013, as set out and discussed in Chapter 2, may change this perception in time.

5. In addition to the perception of expensive court fees, many directors and their advisors remain unaware of how an examinership is paid for; for example, that there is no requirement for funds to be available to pay the examiner's fees 'up front', as the costs of the process are typically funded from new investment, fresh borrowing, a trading surplus or sale of assets at the very end of the protection period. One way or another, a view has persisted among accountants and lawyers in Ireland that examinership is a process for large companies only. In reality, the vast majority of petitions in recent years have been for SMEs. When a company meets the criteria, the High Court has demonstrated a disposition to appointing examiners, regardless of the size of the business, as we shall see in Chapter 4.

6. A continuing hostility among certain sections of the secured creditor community to the examinership process has hindered its more widespread adoption, as illustrated, for example, by the case of *McInerney Contracting Limited and McInerney Contracting Dublin Limited* (known collectively as 'McInerney Homes') in 2011. Perhaps understandably, banks have difficulty in accepting that their normally unassailable

fixed-charge security can, in certain instances, be compromised by an examiner's scheme of arrangement, particularly where those banks are headquartered in jurisdictions that do not have a business recovery process comparable to examinership. Banks also fear the professional costs of the process, which, under the Companies Act 2014, rank ahead of a bank's fixed charge. However, the compulsory 'cramming down' of secured debt (to use the inelegant expression from the US Chapter 11 process) in the teeth of a secured creditor's opposition remains very rare (though, in Chapter 9, we will analyse cases where this has happened).

It seems likely that objections from secured creditors to compulsory write-downs of their debt will continue in both Ireland and Cyprus for the foreseeable future, as lenders invariably want to control whatever insolvency process occurs. This will often mean a receivership and subsequent liquidation of the company.

Examinership in an International Context

Most modern economies have formal corporate recovery processes of one form or another, including economies based on Anglo-Saxon legal principles.

The United States

The Irish examinership process is most closely aligned to the US court process that is set out in Chapter 11 of the United States Bankruptcy Code. Both examinership and the Chapter 11 process take a 'debtor-in-possession' approach, i.e. management remain in control of the business as it is being restructured. While the appointment of an 'examiner' at the request of a creditor in a Chapter 11 case is possible, the role of that examiner is generally quite limited. Under US law, an examiner is authorised to perform investigatory functions and is required to file in court a report of any investigation conducted.

In the US, the state bankruptcy courts have the authority to determine the duties of the examiner in each particular case. If required to do so by the court, an examiner may also carry out any other duties that the court orders the debtor-in-possession (management) not to perform (i.e. the court can prohibit the management/owner from performing certain tasks, and order the examiner to do these tasks instead). In some cases, the examiner may file a plan of reorganisation, negotiate or help the parties negotiate, or review the debtor's schedules of monies owed to determine whether some of the claims are improperly categorised, duties which all have strong echoes in the Irish examinership process. A US examiner may also be directed to determine if objections to any proofs of claim should be filed, or whether causes of action have sufficient merit so that further legal action should be taken.

Under the Chapter 11 process, it is also possible for a creditor to seek the appointment of a 'trustee' who is responsible for the management of the property of the insolvent business, operation of the trade and, if appropriate, the filing of a plan of reorganisation. Section 1106 (a)(5) of the US Bankruptcy Code requires the trustee to file a plan "as soon as practicable" or, alternatively, to file a report explaining why a plan will not be filed. The trustee may recommend that the case be converted to another bankruptcy chapter of the Code (such as Chapter 7, which governs liquidation), or that it be dismissed. These provisions are very similar to the provisions in examinership where the examiner takes on executive functions in the company (see Chapter 7 of this book, which covers the role of the examiner in examinership cases).

The United Kingdom

The closest equivalent to examinership in Great Britain and Northern Ireland is the administration process, which is marked more by its differences to examinership than its similarities. An 'administrator' can be appointed by a debenture holder, by the company or by its directors without having to petition the court. Other creditors must petition the court to appoint an administrator. The administrator must act in the interests of all the creditors and attempt to rescue the company as a going concern. If this proves impossible, he or she must work to create the best possible recovery position for the creditors as a whole. One similarity to examinership is that a court protection order can be issued that forbids any form of legal or insolvency action without the court's permission.

The key difference to examinership is that administration law does not include the concept of debtor-in-possession upon which Chapter 11 and examinership are based. An administration will typically result in the director(s)' immediate loss of control of the company during the reorganisation period. The administrator has the power to do anything necessary or expedient for the management of the affairs, business and property of the company.

Another important difference with examinership is that, under administration, secured creditors enjoy an unassailable position regarding the assets covered by their security. This is certainly not the case in the

Irish system, as mentioned above and as discussed in Chapter 9. From a creditors' perspective, the most draconian provisions of examinership legislation mean that even when secured creditors hold the title deeds to a company's assets, they can be forced to write down their debt as part of a legally binding scheme.

Cyprus

The Members States of the EU have a diverse range of insolvency processes, which reflect their different histories and the evolution of their legal systems. Only two countries – Ireland and Cyprus – operate an almost identical examinership process and, although there has yet to be a successful petition in the Cypriot courts, it is very likely that the legal principles that have developed since 1990 in Ireland will be applied by the Cypriot judiciary in any future petitions. Therefore, the content of this book is equally relevant to Cyprus as it is to Ireland.

About this Guide

This book is intended to be a detailed analysis of the practical aspects of examinership, comprehensively referencing legislation and statements of professional insolvency practice, while focussing on the practical aspects of the discipline, including many examples and cases to illustrate the different facets of the process.

The book is divided into 11 chapters:

Chapter 2 deals with the legislative background to examinership and its evolution since 1990. The advantages to a company of restructuring and reorganising under the process are discussed in Chapter 3. What makes a suitable (and unsuitable) candidate for the process is examined in Chapter 4.

Chapters 5 to 9 of the book lead the reader through the stages of examinership and broadly cover all of the practical aspects of the period of court protection, from the court petition right through to the court confirmation of a scheme of arrangement. Chapter 5 deals with the process for the appointment of the examiner, including a description of the detailed legal documentation required to petition the court. This chapter also explains how the petitioner should navigate the court petitioning process and describes in detail what happens at court hearings as the process begins. It also deals with the independent expert's report (IER), which is now the lynchpin of the petition since the requirement was introduced in 1999 that a company demonstrate that it has a 'reasonable prospect of survival' before it can qualify for examinership. This discussion sets out who can be the independent expert and what is required from the IER. Chapter 6 deals with the supervisory role of the court in the process.

Chapter 7 provides a commentary on the many roles that the examiner may be called upon to perform as the examination of the company is conducted, as outside investment is secured and as an agreement with creditors is sought. It also deals with a further role that the examiner may take on: applying to take over executive control of the company. The chapter sets out examples of when this has happened in practice and the reasons that the course of action was deemed necessary. The atmosphere in which the examiner finds himself or herself once within the trading company can often be fraught as shareholders/directors fight for the survival of their business, perhaps against out-and-out hostility from one or more major creditors. We will see in this chapter that directors can sometimes be hopelessly compromised or lose sight of their responsibilities in such a pressurised environment, resulting in circumstances in which the court orders an investigation into irregularities in the insolvent company.

Chapter 8 deals with the investment process that will often be conducted by the examiner in an effort to recapitalise the business and return it to solvency; Chapter 9 describes the proposals for a scheme of arrangement (or a compromise) with creditors that the examiner is obliged to formulate for the company to emerge from examination. Here we set out how the examiner should go about canvassing the views of the different classes of members and creditors at meetings for that purpose, and how they should report back the consensus view of creditors to the court. We also explain how the scheme of arrangement is confirmed by the court so that it is legally binding on all members and creditors and sets out the grounds on which an objecting party can seek to block the examiner's proposals. Numerous examples explain how parties have succeeded in blocking schemes, including where appeals were taken to the Supreme Court to overturn High Court confirmations, such as the *McInerney Homes*, *Vantive Limited* and *Tivway Limited* Supreme Court cases. Chapter 9 concludes by discussing how a scheme should be implemented in the post-examinership period.

Chapter 10 concerns the costs and remuneration of examiners and their legal advisors, the priority that they enjoy and examples of where the court has intervened in cases where disputes arose regarding costs.

Finally, Chapter 11 offers an analysis of likely future developments regarding examinership, as well as concluding and summarising the book.

The professional accountancy bodies in Ireland have issued guidance to their members through the CCAB-I (the Consultative Committee of Accountancy Bodies in Ireland) and this is provided in Appendix B. Several case studies of successful examinerships (recent at the time of publication) are provided in Appendix A. Finally, Appendix C provides a graphic of the typical timeline for the examinership process.

Throughout *A Practical Guide to Examinership* we have endeavoured to explain the complexities of examinership practice in as much detail as possible in an effort to remove some of the mystique that still surrounds the process and make it far more accessible. Our intention is that in reading and referring to this book, you can easily identify when a company fits the criteria for examinership.

2.
The Development of Examinership

- Introduction
- Background to the Principal Concepts Underpinning Examinership
- Formal Restructuring in Ireland Prior to Examinership
- Introduction of Examinership Legislation: The Goodman Group Crisis
- Examinership Evolving: The 1999 Amendment Act
- National Asset Management Agency Act 2009
- Circuit Court Examinership
- Companies Act 2014
- Examinership Legislation in Cyprus
- Companies (Accounting) Act 2017
- Companies (Miscellaneous Provisions) (Covid-19) Act 2020
- Key Points: The Development of Examinership

Introduction

In this chapter we will look at the background and history of examinership, and the development of the legislative framework that governs the process in both Ireland and Cyprus. In order to understand the reasons why the legislation was first enacted, we will first look at the history of formal restructuring that existed prior to 1990.

Background to the Principal Concepts Underpinning Examinership

The principal practical concepts behind the modern examinership model can be summarised as follows:

- a solution that results in a business remaining a going concern is a preferred outcome for all stakeholders rather than terminating the business;
- a restructuring process will require a period of protection from creditors while claims are frozen throughout the process;
- an independent party is best placed to balance all of the competing interests in a complex trading insolvency case;
- a scheme of arrangement, defined as an agreement with creditors to pay back all, or part of, the company's debts over an agreed timeline, must ultimately become binding on all creditors to ensure that a cohort of 'hold-outs' do not hold the process to ransom.

These fundamental concepts have their roots in changes in commercial law that occurred in the middle of the nineteenth century in the United States and England, which were driven by a series of large-scale insolvency cases relating to railroad companies.

By 1870, no fewer than 14 major railroads in the US were in crisis, insolvent and on the brink of closure. England faced a similar crisis. Faced with hordes of creditors pressing their individual claims and threatening to dismantle functioning railroads, the American and English courts began to establish new laws and insolvency procedures to deal with the looming crisis. Prior to this, corporate insolvency typically meant that a business would close and its assets be sold for the benefit of its creditors. US legislators began to realise that the assets of important pieces of infrastructure, such as railroads, were not readily realisable, especially when the entire sector was in crisis, and that a going concern solution would prove vastly superior to a winding up of the company. Accordingly, the progenitor of the legislation that is now Chapter 11 of the US Corporate Legal Code was introduced, which allowed a business breathing space from creditor claims while it could reorganise and restructure with a view to entering into a compromise scheme with those creditors.

Formal Restructuring in Ireland Prior to Examinership

Prior to 29 August 1990, the only Irish legislation that provided limited formal protection to a business in difficulty were the reorganisation provisions of section 201 of the Companies Act 1963 ('section 201'). While the section 201 process did provide for a compromise of debts between a company and its creditors, the legislation was very rarely used in practice due to a general lack of understanding of the section and in the absence of any clear guidance. (The reorganisation provisions of the old section 201 have since been incorporated in section 449 of the Companies Act 2014.)

While there are certainly similarities between the old section 201 and modern examinership legislation, under section 201 there was no comprehensive protection from creditors to provide breathing space or automatic restriction on the appointment of a receiver. As discussed throughout this book, examinership provides a maximum of 100 days court protection during which no creditor can take legal action against the company in relation to outstanding debts. This also applies in the case where a secured creditor wishes to appoint a receiver; they cannot do so during the examinership process. These provisions did not form part of the 1963 Act. Also, in practical terms it was difficult for the directors of a company to negotiate with a large number of creditors without an independent officer acting and guiding the directors through the process. The 2014 Act now provides a structure for how the process should be conducted. Under the 1963 Act, each class of creditor was required to approve the scheme of arrangement and the level of support required from creditors under this process was higher than that now required under the examinership process, all of which imposed a greater barrier to success for a proposed scheme. In practical terms, the opposition of creditors is the key challenge to successfully implementing a scheme of arrangement, as we will see in Chapter 9.

Introduction of Examinership Legislation: The Goodman Group Crisis

The legislation introducing examinership in Ireland was the Companies (Amendment) Act 1990 ('the 1990 Act') enacted by the Oireachtas on 29 August 1990 after Dáil Éireann was recalled during the summer recess for the first time in 14 years. The requirement to recall the Dáil at the time is a clear indication of the extraordinary circumstances in which this legislation was passed (see below). In Ireland, primary legislation is put forward in the form of a Bill to be passed as an Act or statute by the Irish legislature, the Oireachtas, which is made up of Dáil Éireann (the Dáil), the lower house and principal chamber, and Seanad Éireann (the Seanad), the upper house, as well as the President of Ireland. The 1990 Act originated in the provisions relating to the form of corporate protection for companies first included in Part IX of the Companies (No. 2) Bill 1987. This part of the Bill was subject to almost 50 government amendments in the Seanad before it was finally passed in May 1990.

It is clear from a review of the Oireachtas Committee debates about the Bill in May 1990 that there was a general consensus among all political parties that the provisions were a positive and necessary development, though there were also concerns in relation to the examinership process. John Bruton TD, then deputy leader of the Opposition and later Taoiseach, raised concerns that the Bill did not provide any means for companies using the new process to raise the funding required to trade during the protection period, referencing what was once "the availability of easy or soft money" from the now defunct state lending agency, Foir Teoranta. As discussed later in this book, funding for schemes of arrangement is still a key issue in examinership.

In the original draft of the Bill, it was envisaged that a receiver could be removed by the appointment of an examiner at any time up to 14 days following the receiver's appointment. During the course of the debates on the Bill it was argued that 14 days was a barrier to a receiver properly carrying out their duties, as the possibility of a subsequent appointment of an examiner existed for a period of two weeks. It was agreed to amend this period to seven days, and at the time of finalising the legislation, this period was further reduced to **three** days. (Interestingly, the Cypriot Parliament adopted a much longer timeframe of 30 days when introducing examinership in Cyprus in 2015.)

In 2014, I had the opportunity to interview Des O'Malley TD, who was Minister for Industry and Commerce and instrumental in the introduction of the examinership legislation in 1990. During the interview, Mr O'Malley recalled the circumstances and febrile atmosphere that existed at the time of the introduction of examinership, which was just after the outbreak of the First Gulf War. One of Ireland's largest corporates, the Goodman Group, a meat-processing company, was on the brink of collapse, in part due to an inability to recover debts due from Iraq.

> "[Charles Haughey] told me that Goodman was about to go under and that he'd have to be saved because he employed thousands and thousands of people ... it would have had an appalling effect on the country, the whole economy if Goodman failed because of the thousands employed. He said that he had been thinking about how to handle this and that there was a part or a chapter of the Companies Bill as it then was, 1990, dealing with examinership, which was a new concept for Ireland based on what was known as 'Chapter 11' in the United States and if that part was taken out of the main Bill it could be enacted on its own as a separate standalone Act."

Des O'Malley continued to explain how and why what became the Companies (Amendment) Act 1990 was accelerated through the Oireachtas and was passed into law so quickly:

> "It was to preserve employment, that was the primary concern and that's how Haughey sold it to me as there were thousands of people employed by Goodman. The objective was to try and get the thing resolved one way or another within a reasonable period of time because so many things in this country drag on interminably."

Examinership Evolving: The 1999 Amendment Act

Following the enactment of the 1990 Act, there were consistent calls for amendments to the legislation which, as discussed above, had been enacted in extraordinary circumstances. Although there was an acknowledgment that the original legislation required modification, it was not until 1999 that the legislation was amended.

The Companies (Amendment) (No. 2) Act 1999 ('the 1999 Act') came into effect on 1 February 2000. The main change to the 1990 Act was that more evidence would be required by the court in determining whether to place a company under its protection. Other important changes included and involved:

- a shortened time period for examinations from three months to 70 days, with a possible extension to 100 days;
- the priority enjoyed in relation to expenses certified by the examiner, whereby the examiner can certify a debt during the period of examinership that if the company went into liquidation following

the examinership, this debt would have priority in line with the examiner's costs;

- removal of the shareholder veto on schemes of arrangement;
- introduction of the right of set-off for financial institutions (allowing them to claim funds on hand from a company in the event of examinership); and
- strengthening of the position of leaseholders.

We consider some of the most fundamental amendments below.

First, and most importantly, the 1999 Act raised the bar in respect of the criteria for a company entering into the examinership process. The 'reasonable prospect of survival' test was introduced for the first time. Previously, the legislation allowed the court to appoint an examiner if the court considered "that such order would be likely to facilitate the survival of the company". This was amended by the 1999 Act to include an onus on there being a reasonable prospect of survival for a company to be granted the protection of the court:

> "The Court shall not make an order under this section unless it is satisfied that there is a reasonable prospect of the survival of the company."[1]

This was a fundamental shift and the reasonable prospect of survival test still remains the cornerstone of any court petition to appoint an examiner. We will discuss in Chapter 9 the kinds of contentious arguments that have been put forward by various parties in order to prove or disprove whether a company has a reasonable prospect of survival.

Under section 19 of the 1990 Act, there was a requirement for an examiner to report back to the court within 21 days setting out results of meetings, recommendations of creditors, amounts owed to creditors and the examiner's recommendations regarding how to move forward. This section was removed by the 1999 Act, shifting the requirement to provide certain information to the court in respect of the company to the pre-petition stage, in the form of an independent accountant's report (IAR), now known as the independent expert's report (IER). Under the original 1990 legislation, the examiner was obliged to focus initially on determining if the company could survive or not. The independent expert, who is often the company's auditor, but can also be an independent qualified accountant or auditor, now provides the opinion as to whether a company has a reasonable prospect of survival, rather than the examiner.

---

[1] Companies (Amendment) (No. 2) Act, 1999. Amendment of Section 2 of Act of 1990.

The practical impact of the 1999 amendments meant that work normally carried out by the examiner in the initial 21 days of the appointment now had to be carried out prior to the petition being presented to the court. Therefore, there would still be the risk of a receiver being appointed before the petition for examinership could be granted as a company struggled to commission an IER in time. Earlier in this chapter, we mentioned the debate surrounding the provision relating to the period in which a receiver could stand appointed, and a petition for examinership still be presented, noting that this period initially stood at 14 days but was reduced to three. In practical terms, while it has proved difficult since 1999 for companies to successfully petition the court when a receiver is already in place, it has certainly not been impossible and there have been examples in more recent years where a receiver was forced to stand down by the presentation of a petition to appoint an examiner. For example in June 2012, a petition to appoint an examiner was made by the company in the case of *Clane Inn Limited*, a hotel and pub business based in County Kildare, where the receiver was ordered to stand down when the petition was granted.

Secondly, while the 1990 Act provided that the initial period of protection was up to three months, the 1999 Act shortened this time period to 70 days, though the 1999 Act also allowed for the period of protection to be extended for a further 30 days if such an extension will enable the examiner to put proposals for a compromise and scheme of arrangement to the company's members and creditors. In Cyprus, the legislation allows for a more generous initial period of four months, which can be extended up to six months.

Thirdly, the restriction on the right of set-off that existed in respect of financial institutions under the 1990 Act was removed under the 1999 Act. This treatment of financial institutions was considered unfair because it only applied to a specific type of creditor. For example, a supplier who enjoyed a right of set-off between a creditor and debtor account held with a company could retain that right, meaning that any write-off of debt under a scheme of arrangement would not apply to the credit balance only and had to take into account the right of set-off.

Fourthly, and as mentioned above, under the 1990 Act the examiner could certify liabilities that were necessary for the survival of the company, and these liabilities would rank as expenses of the examinership in any winding-up or receivership, thereby ranking ahead of the fixed-charge holder in relation to realisations from assets subject to such a charge. This became a powerful tool for examiners in ensuring, for example, continuity of supply, as the protection to suppliers, whose costs were certified by the examiner, extended to an effective first charge on the fixed assets of the company, which would otherwise only be available to a secured creditor on a winding-up.

The 1999 Act amended the priority of expenses certified by the examiner to rank below fixed security on a winding-up. This amendment, while understandable for the protection of fixed security, has significantly diminished the value of what are now known as 'Section 529 certificates' under the Companies Act 2014. These certificates can be given by the examiner to suppliers to encourage them to continue trading with the company while it is under court protection. They are dealt with in detail in Chapter 7, The Role of the Examiner. Though certified examinership creditors remain near the top of the queue in any subsequent winding up, the certificate only has value if there are floating assets (e.g. stock, debtors or cash) to meet the certificate.

National Asset Management Agency Act 2009

The next development in examinership came with the establishment of the National Asset Management Agency (NAMA) under the National Asset Management Agency Act 2009 ('NAMA Act 2009'). NAMA was established "to address a serious threat to the economy and to the systemic stability of credit institutions in the State generally". It did this by removing the bad loans from each of the systemic Irish banks and housing them with the new agency to be managed and for security to be realised.

As discussed above, a receiver can be removed within the first three days of their appointment under the 1990 Act. However, section 150 of the NAMA Act 2009 provides that a statutory receiver cannot be displaced by the appointment of an examiner. In the case of *Tougher's Oil Distributors Limited* (2012), a petition for examinership was presented by the company, which was a fuel distribution and property development business in Kildare. As part of the petition, an interim examiner was sought. As required, the petitioner confirmed that it had obligations in relation to a bank asset (as defined by the NAMA Act 2009) that had been transferred to NAMA or a NAMA group entity. However, NAMA had not been put on notice of the presentation of the petition. An interim examiner was appointed to the company and the petitioner put NAMA on notice of a further hearing to confirm the appointment of the examiner. At the further hearing, counsel for NAMA argued that the interim examiner had not been validly appointed because, pursuant to section 2(5) of the NAMA Act 2009, NAMA was required to be put on notice and heard on the matter prior to the appointment of an examiner. Mr Justice Peter Charleton ruled in favour of NAMA on this point, ruling that the interim examiner had not been validly appointed. He did, however, subsequently appoint an examiner and the company emerged successfully from the process in February 2013.

Circuit Court Examinership

From the outset it has been intended that examinership for smaller companies would be accessible in the Circuit Court rather than just the High Court to allow costs to be reduced and to encourage the use of the process. Section 3(9)(a) of the 1990 Act stated:

> "Where it appears to the court that the total liabilities of the company (taking into account its contingent and prospective liabilities) do not exceed £250,000, the court may, after making such interim or other orders as it thinks fit, order that the matter be remitted to the judge of the Circuit Court in whose circuit the company has its registered office or principal place of business."

In practice, Circuit Court examinership was unheard of before the case of *Celbridge Play Zone Limited*, a Kildare-based company that went into examinership in 2014. This case marked the first occasion that an examiner was appointed outside the High Court when Judge Gerard Griffin in Naas Circuit Court appointed an examiner to the company. Celbridge Play Zone Limited went on to successfully emerge from the process.

The first significant sign of any real change in this regard came in November 2012 with the announcement by then Minister for Jobs, Enterprise and Employment, Richard Bruton TD, of the intention to amend the 1990 Act to allow SMEs to apply directly to the Circuit Court for examinership. Under the Companies (Miscellaneous Provisions) Act 2013, a company was eligible to apply to the Circuit Court to avail of the protection of examination if it met two of the following three conditions applied:
- balance sheet did not exceed €4.4 million;
- turnover of less than €8.8 million;
- number of employees did not exceed 50.

These conditions are in turn drawn directly from the European Commission's definition of an SME (as set out in Commission Recommendation 2003/361/EC of 6 May 2003).

The introduction of this SME-friendly examinership process has resulted in dozens of Circuit Court examinership cases since 2013 and the two of the three criteria have subsequently been broadened, as set out in the section on the Companies (Accounting) Act 2017 below.

Companies Act 2014

The next evolutionary step came with the consolidation and development of all Irish companies legislation into Companies Act 2014, including the examinership legislation, i.e. the 1990 Act (as amended by the 1999 and 2009 Acts). There were minor technical changes only to the examinership provisions at this stage.

Examinership Legislation in Cyprus

The Cypriot Companies Legislation was amended in the summer of 2015 following the near collapse of the Cypriot economy and is heavily reliant upon the examinership provisions of the Irish Companies Act. The only significant changes were that:
1. a receiver could stand appointed for 30 days, rather than the three days under Irish law; and
2. an examinership could have an overall possible length of six months, as compared to 100 days in Ireland.

For all intents and purposes, however, the examinership processes in both Ireland and Cyprus are identical.

Companies (Accounting) Act 2017

The Companies Act 2014 provided for a priority system for claims of different classes of a company's creditors in the event of its insolvency. The claims of fixed charge holders ranked first, followed by those of preferential creditors, floating charge holders and, lastly, unsecured creditors. Prior to implementation of the Companies (Accounting) Act 2017 ('the 2017 Act'), case law dictated that crystallisation of floating charges into fixed charges afforded priority to secured lenders over the claims of preferential creditors. This was held to be so in the Supreme Court decision in the 2015 case of *J.D. Brian Limited (in liquidation) t/a East Coast Print and Publicity*.

The 2017 Act amended certain provisions of the 2014 Act:
- to provide that claims of preferential creditors now rank in priority to those of floating charges. This priority applies irrespective of the prior crystallisation of floating charges into fixed charges;
- any receiver appointed under a floating charge that has crystallised into a fixed charge must now ensure that claims of preferential creditors are paid in priority to those of the charge holder.

Finally, pursuant to the 2017 Act, in order to avail of Circuit Court examinership, the company must meet two of the following criteria:
- balance sheet does not exceed €6 million;
- annual turnover does not exceed €12 million;
- number of employees does not exceed 50.

Companies (Miscellaneous Provisions) (Covid-19) Act 2020

The primary purpose of this Act is to provide for interim measures and for temporary amendments to the Companies Act 2014 to deal with the impact of the Covid-19 pandemic. In normal circumstances, the examiner of an Irish company has 70 days to provide a report to the court, which may be extended by 30 days to 100 days in exceptional circumstances. However, under this Act, an additional extension period of 50 days is provided for, which means, where the court is satisfied that it is warranted by exceptional circumstances related to the pandemic, an examiner may be afforded up to 150 days to present their report (i.e. 70 + 30 + 50 days). This increases the period of court protection for such a company. The additional 50 days can only be applied for after Day 70.

KEY POINTS: THE DEVELOPMENT OF EXAMINERSHIP

1. The fundamental concepts of examinership have their roots in changes in commercial law that occurred in the middle of the nineteenth century in the US and England, following large-scale insolvency cases in the railroad industry.
2. Prior to 1990, section 201 of the Companies Act 1963 was the only legislation in Ireland which provided formal protection to businesses facing difficulties. The reorganisation provisions of the 'old' section 201 have been incorporated in section 449 of the Companies Act 2014.

3. The Companies (Amendment) Act 1990 introduced examinership into Irish law and the first company to enter examinership was one of Ireland's largest companies, the Goodman Group.
4. The legislation evolved in the Companies (Amendment) (No. 2) Act 1999, which required that more evidence be provided to the court for it to determine whether to place a company under its protection. The time period for court protection was shortened from three months to 70 days (with a possible extension to 100 days).
5. The 1999 Act introduced the 'reasonable prospect of survival' test, which remains the cornerstone of any court petition to appoint an examiner. The opinion as to whether a company has a reasonable prospect of survival is presented by an independent qualified accountant or auditor in the form of an independent expert's report (IER).
6. The 1999 Act also removed the restriction on the right of set-off that existed in respect of financial institutions.
7. The Companies (Miscellaneous Provisions) Act 2013 made examinership more accessible for SMEs as they could apply to the Circuit Court rather than the High Court if they satisfied two of the following conditions: their balance sheet assets did not exceed €4.4 million, turnover did not exceed €8.8 million and/or they employed less than 50 staff.
8. These conditions were amended by the Companies (Accounting) Act 2017. In order to avail of Circuit Court examinership, the company must meet two of the following criteria: its balance sheet does not exceed €6 million, its annual turnover does not exceed €12 million and/or it employs less than 50 staff.

3.
The Benefits of Examinership

- Introduction
- Protection from Creditors
- Job Protection
- Intangible Assets are Maintained
- Repudiation of Onerous Contracts
- Transparency and Certainty for Investors
- Mechanism for Creditors to Restore Proper Controls
- Mechanism to Adjudicate Creditors' Claims
- Savings for the State
- Creditors Cannot Be Unfairly Prejudiced
- Some Downsides to Examinership
- Key Points: The Benefits of Examinership

Introduction

In this chapter we will explain some of the practical benefits, and also some of the disadvantages of the examinership process. It is clear that a major benefit of the examinership legislation is intended to be the preservation of jobs at risk. As previously discussed in Chapter 1, the onus of court protection has been primarily focused on retaining and saving jobs in viable enterprises that are insolvent or on the brink of insolvency and that would otherwise be lost. As stated by Mr Justice Barrett in the 2014 case of *JP Transpeed Express Portlaoise Limited* (reminiscent of the statement of Chief Justice Frank Clarke in the 2007 *Traffic Group Limited* case):

> "We are fortunate to live in a republic which, to quote Lincoln when speaking of the United States, enjoys 'government of the people, by the people, for the people'. So, it is perhaps not surprising that the people's representatives in the Oireachtas should have established a system of examinership that has at its heart a consideration, amongst other matters, of the fate of so-called 'ordinary' people, in particular those workers whose continuing employment prospects have been rendered uncertain by the fact that their employer has gone into examinership and may yet enter into liquidation. There is relatively recent case law which supports the conclusion that the future employment prospects of such workers are an issue of real importance when it comes to examinership-related applications."

Additionally, to borrow a phrase from economists, the 'multiplier effect' of the loss of jobs in one business could have wider and equally serious implications for jobs in other, related enterprises in the general community. An example of this phenomenon occurred in January 2018 following the collapse of the UK construction giant Carillion during a boom in that sector. There ensued a sharp increase in the number of construction-related companies seeking court protection in Ireland, with nine companies from the sector having petitioned the court for examinership. The Carillion example demonstrates the wider effect that one insolvency event can have on an entire industry and the people employed by it.

Protection from Creditors

Following the successful presentation of its petition to appoint an examiner, the company is often referred to as being 'under the protection of the court', with the period of examination being referred to as the 'protection period'. While the company is in examinership or during the protection period:

- no proceedings for winding up of the company may be commenced, nor can a resolution be passed for its winding up;
- no receiver may be appointed to the company or any of its assets;
- no attachment or execution may be put into force against the property of the company, except with the consent of the examiner;
- where a debt is secured by way of mortgage, charge, lien or other encumbrance or pledge, no action may be taken to realise the whole or any part of that security, except with the consent of the examiner;
- no steps may be taken to repossess goods in the company's possession under any lease or hire-purchase agreement, except with the consent of the examiner;
- where personal guarantees are provided by the directors or shareholders of the company (or indeed any other party), no proceedings may be commenced against the personal guarantors while the company is under the protection of the court, thus affording the same protection to the personal guarantors as that afforded to the company. This protection also extends to corporate guarantors.

Therefore, examinership is a powerful and highly beneficial tool for a company that is insolvent or about to become insolvent as it affords the company time and breathing space in which to restructure its balance sheet. This protection period can last up to 100 days in Ireland (up to six months in Cyprus).

For example, as we will see in Chapter 7, while under the protection of the court, a debenture holder, such as a bank, cannot appoint a receiver, a creditor cannot initiate legal proceedings against the company, the Revenue Sheriff cannot seize goods, and creditors that have supplied goods to the company on a retention-of-title basis cannot seek to have their goods returned. All such creditor claims will be dealt with by the examiner in the scheme of arrangement to be formulated, which we will explore further in Chapter 9.

Examinership vs the Section 450 Restructuring Process

Under Part 9 of the Companies Act 2014, section 450 provides for an alternative process whereby a company can agree a formal scheme of arrangement with members and creditors. While there are certainly

similarities between the section 450 process and the examinership provisions, the following is a summary of the key differences:
- under the examinership legislation, the protection period affords a
  company protection from its creditors, unlike a formal compromise
  or arrangement with members and creditors pursuant to section 450;
- there is no time limit by which to conclude the section 450 process,
  whereas a limit of 100 days applies in examinership, which provides
  more certainty to the process;
- under the section 450 process, there is reduced involvement by the
  court as court approval is not necessary to convene meetings of
  members and creditors (such meetings are convened by the directors
  of the company);
- unlike examinership, the section 450 process provides no automatic
  restriction on the appointment of a receiver, unless the company
  incurs the costs necessary to make an application to the court to place
  a stay on all proceedings against the company;
- most importantly, a 'special majority' of 75% support in value of
  creditor classes imposes a higher barrier to success for a proposed
  section 450 scheme. By comparison, in examinership the creditors are divided into classes by the examiner and the threshold for
  support within each class is 50%. Additionally, the section 450 process demands special majority support from **every** class of creditor
  impacted by the scheme of arrangement, whereas only one class of
  impaired creditor is required in an examinership for a scheme to be
  capable of being brought before the court for approval.

In Cyprus, the formal restructuring process is similar to that in Ireland.
However, one advantage the Cypriot legislation has over the Irish
equivalent is that only a simple majority of 50% of the creditors present
and voting is required in order to approve a scheme of arrangement.

In practice, it is often difficult for directors of a company to negotiate
with a large number of creditors and as each class of creditor is required
to approve the scheme of arrangement, examinership has been favoured
over the section 450 process since its introduction in 1990.

When comparing the examinership process with the section 450 process, perhaps the most striking differentiator is that examinership is the
only viable option to protect a company with a prospect of survival
when faced with a secured creditor seeking to enforce their security.
For example, following the appointment of a receiver, or a receiver and
manager, by a debenture holder, the examinership legislation allows a
company to present a petition to appoint an examiner, thereby removing the receiver (within three days of the appointment of a receiver in

Ireland and 30 days of the appointment of a receiver and manager in Cyprus).

In the 2017 example of *Edward Holdings Group* (a group of companies operating two Galway hotels, a business park and a cinema), the group sought the appointment of an examiner following the appointment of a receiver to a number of companies within the group. The appointment of the receiver took place on a Friday afternoon. The petition papers in this case were presented to the judge on Saturday afternoon, and the initial examinership hearing took place on the following Monday. This group of companies successfully emerged from examinership in December 2017. A similar set of circumstances occurred with *Regan Development Limited* in February 2017, which involved the successful examinership of the Regency Hotel in Dublin and the 2012 *Clane Inn Limited* case, which involved the Maudlins House Hotel in County Kildare.

Job Protection

As already highlighted in the introduction to this chapter, a key intention behind the examinership legislation is the preservation of jobs in viable enterprises that would otherwise be lost. Thousands of jobs have been retained through examinership in all types of industries, from very large companies and household names like Eircom and Ladbrokes to much smaller companies in rural locations across Ireland.

An example of a smaller company in a rural location being a very strong candidate for examinership was *Frenchpark Service Station Limited*, which operated a service station and convenience store in Frenchpark, County Roscommon, and which went successfully through the examinership process in 2016. There were many factors leading to the company's insolvency, including substantial tax and rent liabilities. While the company had only eight employees, four full time and four part time, the value of these jobs and the services that the business provided to the local community was significant. If the company had been placed into liquidation or ceased to trade, then local people would have been required to travel 15 to 20 minutes (approximately 25 kilometres) to the nearest town in order to buy groceries and fuel. This examinership demonstrated the positive impact the process can have on one community, especially the benefits of preserving an important business for that community.

It is often argued by creditors, however, and particularly secured creditors, that following the appointment of a receiver, employment within the business will be retained through the continued trading of the company under the receiver or the disposal of the company as a going concern. However, as argued in previous chapters, this is of little comfort to long-standing employees who may be replaced by other employees following the business sale. Examinership is focused on preserving the *jobs of people* employed by the business, not the *roles* that may exist within a future incarnation of the business. In addition, the transfer of undertakings protection of employment (TUPE) regulations may not protect employees where there has been a short cessation in the employment following the appointment of a receiver or a disposal of the business, as discussed in Chapter 1.

Intangible Assets are Maintained

As discussed above, the company comes under the protection of the court following the presentation of a petition for the appointment of an examiner, which protects the company's assets from its creditors during the period of examinership. These assets are the typical assets one would expect to see on a company's balance sheet, such as fixtures and fittings, machinery, debtors, stock, cash, etc. However, the protection of the court also extends to the company's intangible assets, such as intellectual property from research and development, customer lists and contracts. These are assets that are not always captured by the company's balance sheet but are of significant value to the operations of the business as a going concern.

The construction industry is one in which the protection afforded under examinership to a company's intangible assets is prevalent. Many of the contracts that construction companies have in place with their clients will usually include an insolvency clause, which means that in an insolvency event, such as on the appointment of a liquidator or a receiver, the client may immediately cancel the contract. However, if the company is placed into examinership, the contract can usually be maintained through negotiations between the examiner and the client, which will have benefits for both the company and the client as the company receives the balance of the sums due under contract and maintains employment, while the client still receives the contracted services.

Restructuring professionals have seen many construction company insolvencies, either through liquidation or receivership, where there has been a footrace among creditors of the insolvent company, meaning that they have sought to recover what they can from the company through any means possible, such as removing assets or stock from sites, which then results in complex issues for the appointed liquidator or receiver in order to realise those assets. If a liquidator or receiver is appointed in the case of a construction company insolvency, the clients of that company will ultimately be asked to fund the completion of their contracted projects, whereas if the company is placed into examinership it can complete the projects from cash flows remaining to be received on those projects. Therefore, an examinership in the construction industry generally provides a better outcome for all stakeholders than other processes.

By way of example, in late 2016, the *Walsh Mechanical Group* entered examinership as a result of losses on specific contracts. The group of companies forming part of the petition included a mechanical engineering and ducting company engaged on several contracts across Ireland. Following the appointment of an examiner, discussions and meetings were held with all clients for projects the group was engaged on. This allowed the group to remain engaged in and finish out the contracts for these clients. While the company lost one contract during the protection period, it was not detrimental to the overall operations of the group as the contract in question was loss-making and onerous. Through the examinership process the company was in a position to cancel the onerous contract with the client, leading to them having a claim for damages included in the scheme of arrangement, without the company having to initiate repudiation of contract proceedings in court.

Examinership is the only business recovery mechanism through which a company can repudiate onerous contracts. This is discussed in more detail in the next section.

Repudiation of Onerous Contracts

A company in examinership can seek the approval of the court to repudiate a part or all of an onerous contract in order to facilitate the survival of the company as a whole. Following presentation of the company's application, the court may determine the amount of any such loss or damage suffered by the creditor as a result of the repudiation of the onerous contract for inclusion in the examiner's scheme of arrangement. Where the examiner is not a party to the application for examinership, the company shall also serve notice to the examiner so that they may appear and be heard at the repudiation hearing.

The option to repudiate contracts under examinership was commonly used by multi-unit retailers who were paying excessive rents during the 2008–2012 recession. A high profile example is the *Debenhams* examinership in the summer of 2016, where the company sought to repudiate a number of its leases to allow for the survival of the company as a whole. In Ireland, Debenhams' leases included 'upward-only' clauses, which were commonplace during the 'Celtic Tiger' years (later banned by section 132 of the Land and Conveyancing Law Reform Act 2009). This meant that though the company's turnover and profits had decreased, the rent it was paying to its landlords could only go up, thus crippling the business with unsustainable operational costs. Regrettably, the company only managed to trade for a further four years before entering liquidation in 2020 as a result of the Covid-19 crisis.

The option to repudiate a lease can also be used by the examiner and the company during the protection period as a powerful negotiating tool with the company's landlords. This was the case in the 2012 examinership of the *Deerhaven Group*, a greeting-cards retailer, based in Limerick. The company operated from seven shopping centre units across Ireland and traded profitably for many years before becoming loss-making following the onset of the economic recession. Once again, the critical issue it faced was being tied into onerous, long-term, upwards-only leases at far-above-market terms. All other variable costs of the business were successfully reduced in line with its turnover, but the company was unable to reduce its main overhead: rent. The company entered examinership and the weakest trading store was immediately closed. Negotiations took place with landlords using the examinership framework and reductions of rents payable of between 50% and 80% were achieved. These reductions were sufficient to turn around the company's fortunes and render it profitable. The effect of the company's option to repudiate the lease was evident in this examinership. Even though an examinership cannot compel a landlord to re-write the terms of a lease, it is safe to assume that the landlords knew it would be more advantageous for them to agree a reduced rent with the company instead of having a vacant unit generating no income, given that the demand for commercial units in 2012 was low. Having been a critical issue for retail and restaurant business in the recession following the Celtic Tiger years, the Covid-19 crisis of 2020 brought the issue of excessive rents centre stage once again.

The option to repudiate contracts can also be used for other purposes. For example, it can be used to repudiate service contracts that have become onerous. This was seen in the 2017 examinership of *FCR Media Ltd*, the operating company for the Golden Pages business listings directory, where, during the due diligence phase (i.e. an investor's 'deep dive' into the company's books and records – see Chapter 8), the proposed investor identified a number of onerous service agreements the company had with its clients. The investor did not wish to take on these contracts as part of the entity to emerge from the examinership, which led to the company requesting approval from the court to repudiate the service contracts. This request was granted by the court as it was necessary for the formulation of the scheme of arrangement by the examiner. The clients' claims for damages were included in the examiner's scheme of arrangement (the examiner's scheme of arrangement is discussed in detail in Chapter 9). If the service contracts had not been repudiated, the investor would have removed their interest, meaning that the examiner would not have been in a position to formulate a scheme of arrangement and the company would have been placed into liquidation.

Transparency and Certainty for Investors

As mentioned above and discussed in more detail in Chapters 7 and 8, the examiner often carries out a search for an investor to fund a scheme of arrangement that will allow the company to exit the examinership process successfully. During this process, the examiner will also verify and check all creditors' claims and balances. This provides certainty to investors in respect of liabilities, if any, being assumed and how their investment will be divided among the various classes of creditors. It also provides the investor with comfort that the company that they will be taking over will be asset-rich, with the only preferential and unsecured liabilities surviving being those incurred during the protection period. In normal corporate finance transactions, investors can often take on substantial risk in respect of a company's liabilities, whether they are known or unknown at the time of investment. When investing in a company through an examinership, however, the scheme of arrangement formulated by the examiner clearly sets out liabilities as at the petition date that will be written down and often includes a 'post-examinership' balance sheet that sets out the financial position of the company immediately after the conclusion of the examinership. This is of particular benefit to external investors.

The examinership process can also allow existing directors or shareholders to invest either equity or indeed loan capital to the company in order to fund the examiner's scheme of arrangement. These funds can often be arranged in conjunction with investment from an external third party. The repayment of such loan capital from either existing or new investors is usually subordinated under the scheme of arrangement to any payments due under the scheme. When the cash reserves of the company allow for repayment of such loans advanced, they can be repaid tax free to the director or shareholder, therefore providing a potentially tax-efficient way in which to invest and withdraw funds from a company. It is important to note that in recent years, the High Court has given extra scrutiny to investments made predominately as loans from existing directors or shareholders and it is the examiner's duty to ensure that the company is sufficiently capitalised in order to survive as a going concern post examinership, continue to trade profitably and thereby service such loans.

Mechanism for Creditors to Restore Proper Controls

As discussed throughout this book, there are a number of parties who can petition the court for the appointment of an examiner, one of these being a creditor of the company. There have been a number of examples over the years where creditors have sought the appointment of an examiner, for example the petition by Sony for the appointment of an examiner to *Golden Discs Limited* in 2009 and the appointment of an examiner by Beachpoint Capital to *Maximum Media Networks Limited (Joe.ie)* in 2020.

Where a creditor believes that a company can survive as a going concern, but is concerned about the management or governance of the company, it can petition the court for the appointment of an examiner. The examiner can then independently examine the company and establish whether a new management team is required. There is also an option for the examiner to temporarily take over executive functions of the company if they find that the current management are unwilling to cooperate during the protection period. However, it is essential to note that, in practical terms, an examiner working closely with the directors of the company gives the maximum chance of success for the examinership.

Mechanism to Adjudicate Creditors' Claims

In many cases a company may be in *bona fide* dispute with its creditors in respect of liabilities claimed to be owed by the company. Through examinership, however, the company has a mechanism to have these *bona fide* claims adjudicated. In the 2009 examinership of *Ely Medical Group Limited* and related companies, the company disputed the amount that a secured charge creditor claimed. The secured creditor relied on a sum of €2,450,000 in accordance with a loan agreement entered into with the company; the loan was provided to the company in two instalments. The company disputed the first instalment in the amount of €1,250,000 and sought directions from the court during the protection period on the actual sum due. Mr Justice McGovern adjudicated the quantum of the secured debt and concluded that the company's level of secured debt was €1,200,000, plus agreed interest. This resulted in reducing the overall claim of the creditor and formed part of the scheme of arrangement.

As mentioned earlier in this chapter, in 2017 *Regan Development Limited*, which operated the former Regency Hotel in Dublin, entered examinership with a related company. The companies disputed the level of debt owing to a secured creditor and it was not possible for the examiner to adjudicate the level of the debt within the protection period. The examiner, through his scheme of arrangement, provided the company with a mechanism to resolve the issue by appointing an independent expert to adjudicate on the claims of the secured creditor. The scheme was approved by the court with funds held in escrow to deal with the disputed sum due to the secured creditor. The independent expert concluded her report within the specified period provided for under the scheme and a sum was refunded from escrow to the companies, with the expert having sided with the company in examinership on certain of the points made in its claim that the debt was disputed.

In the 2018 case of *Yvolve Sports Limited*, a distributor of children's scooters located in Dublin petitioned the court to appoint an examiner because of a dispute that arose between the shareholders and directors of the company relating to, among other things, sums owed by the company to its investors. During the protection period, the examiner adjudicated on the level of debt. A settlement was reached between the shareholders and the relevant directors prior to the petition being withdrawn (because a settlement had been reached).

Similarly, in *Quesada Developments Limited*, a 2018 examinership case involving a nursing home facility in County Kildare, a dispute existed regarding one of the directors' claims against the company. The scheme of arrangement prepared by the examiner provided the company with a mechanism to resolve the issue by appointing an independent expert to adjudicate on these claims. The scheme was approved by the court and the independent expert finalised his report and concluded the matter within the specified period as set out in the scheme.

Savings for the State

If the examiner is successful in having a scheme of arrangement approved by the court, then there are invariably significant savings for the State, the first of which is in respect of the dividend paid to the Revenue Commissioners through the examiner's proposals. While in some cases these dividends can be disappointing, with Revenue understandably voicing its dissatisfaction with low dividends, the reality is that the dividend payable is always greater than would be the case if the company entered liquidation, where there are very often no funds available for the preferential or unsecured creditors.

The second saving to the State is in respect of employee claims. When a company successfully exits the examinership process, employment within that company is maintained. If the company was instead forced to enter liquidation or receivership, its employees may be made redundant and the Department of Employment Affairs and Social Protection will receive claims from those employees in respect of redundancies, arrears of wages, arrears of holiday pay and notice pay. Clearly, the total sum of such claims will depend on the number of employees involved, their length of service, etc., but there have been cases where this liability has run into many millions of euro.

Creditors Cannot Be Unfairly Prejudiced

When creditors oppose the examiner's proposals they often argue that their rights as creditors are unfairly prejudiced by the implementation of the scheme of arrangement. This means that the opposing creditors believe that they would fare better in a liquidation or receivership of the company. However, as set out in section 541 of the Companies Act 2014:

> "The Court shall not confirm any proposals unless ... the Court is satisfied that the proposals are fair and equitable in relation to any class of members or creditors that has not accepted the proposals whose interests or claims would be impaired by implementation, and the proposals are not unfairly prejudicial to the interests of any interested party."

In effect, the examiner cannot prepare a scheme of arrangement for a company that would result in a worse treatment for its members or creditors than if the company were to be liquidated or placed into receivership. For example, secured creditors must, at a minimum, receive the market value of their security in the examiner's proposals or preferential creditors must receive a dividend greater than that expected in a liquidation.

In some examinerships, it has been argued by creditors, secured creditors in particular, that they would fare better if the scheme of arrangement was not approved. In an examinership in 2011 involving *McInerney Homes*, Anglo Irish Bank produced a report estimating that the bank would benefit more from a long-term receivership of the company than the immediate settlement of its liabilities through the examiner's scheme of arrangement. In this case, the judge decided in favour of the secured creditor and the examiner's proposals were not approved. It should be noted that the onus is on the examiner to put evidence before the court that creditors will not fare better in a liquidation or receivership of the company.

Some Downsides to Examinership

The examinership process is not without certain drawbacks. In order to present a balanced view, a number of common criticisms or disadvantages of the process are discussed below.

Suspension of Creditors' Rights

As we have seen, a company that has successfully presented a petition for examinership is protected from its creditors while the examinership is ongoing. Some creditors of protected companies have argued that the examinership process sterilises their statutory rights. For example, a secured creditor cannot appoint a receiver to its security or seek to transfer or sell its security while a company is in examinership.

Usually, secured creditors are entitled to receive the full market value of their security, though the company in examinership does not have the option to repay the debt over a restructured loan term. In some cases, this has involved the secured creditors writing off a portion of the capital and interest due on the loan. In the examinership of *McInerney Homes* in 2011 (see above), although Mr Justice Clarke refused to confirm the scheme of arrangement proposed by the examiner on the basis that the secured creditor, Anglo Irish Bank, would be unfairly prejudiced, he did make it clear that a secured creditor can be compelled to accept a discount on their loan in an examinership. This has paved the way in recent years for schemes of arrangement that compel secured creditors to accept a sum lower than the balance owed to them, if the value of their security is less than the sum owed, through the examiner's scheme of arrangement. Such schemes were confirmed by the High Court in the *Clane Inn Limited* case in 2012 and by the Circuit Court in the *Com-Plas Packaging Limited and Scriptdale Trading Limited* case in 2017 (although this examinership scheme was never implemented). This always requires detailed valuation evidence of a particular asset to confirm that the value of the security is less than the sum owed.

The Cost of Examinership

In accordance with the legislation, the examiner's remuneration, costs and expenses are paid in priority over any other claim against the company, out of the assets of the company. Section 554 of the Companies Act 2014 states:

> "The remuneration, costs and expenses of an examiner which have been sanctioned by order of the Court … shall be paid in full and shall be paid before any other claim, secured or unsecured, under any compromise or scheme of arrangement or in any receivership or winding up of the company to which he or she has been appointed."

In practice, should the examiner be successful in approving the scheme of arrangement, they will have previously agreed their remuneration, costs and expenses with the proposed investor and the company, and this will be discharged from the investment sum before any dividends are paid to creditors.

If the examinership process is unsuccessful and a liquidator or receiver is appointed, the examiner's remuneration, costs and expenses are paid in priority to any other claim, including that of the receiver's fees, liquidator's fees or amounts due to the secured creditor. If a company has a secured asset with a bank and a receiver is appointed, the receiver is in effect collating and selling the assets of the company in order to first discharge the costs of the preceding unsuccessful examinership and then, secondly, repaying the secured creditor. Many of the criticisms from secured creditors in relation to examinership have centred on the costs of the examinership being paid from the proceeds from the sale of their securities. In liquidations following an unsuccessful examinership, the returns to preferential and unsecured creditors of the company are reduced, as examiner's and liquidator's fees and costs rank ahead of their claims.

If an examinership is successful, however, the preferential and unsecured creditors will receive a dividend greater than they would in a liquidation scenario. In this respect, there are also significant benefits for the unsecured creditors if an examiner's proposals are approved, as they not only receive a dividend, but also can continue to supply the company post examinership and have the benefit of a trading customer into the future.

Low Dividends

At the majority of creditors' meetings held at the end of each examinership to allow the members and creditors to vote on the examiner's scheme of arrangement, many creditors, particularly unsecured creditors, voice their displeasure at the low percentage of outstanding debt being repaid to them. In most cases, this dividend to unsecured creditors can be low, i.e. in single digit percentages ranging from 1% to 10%. This can often be difficult for the creditors to accept as a number of them might have been relying on the payment coming from the company in examinership to meet their own obligations.

However, it is clear that as macroeconomic conditions improve, so too do the average levels of dividends payable in schemes of arrangement. In particular, in the period 2017 to 2020 there was a trend in examinerships whereby all unconnected preferential and unsecured creditors received higher dividends, as much as 100% of the monies they were owed. This occurred in two of the cases discussed above, i.e. the *Regan Development Limited* and *Edward Holdings Group* examinerships, both of which involved secured assets in the hospitality sector. These cases have pointed to an upward trend in respect of the dividend payable to preferential and unsecured creditors in the intervening period between recessions. As the Irish economy grew and generally improved, the value of companies' assets increased, which resulted in increased investment in companies, in turn allowing for better returns to creditors.

KEY POINTS: BENEFITS OF EXAMINERSHIP

1. The primary focus of court protection is to retain and save jobs in viable enterprises that are insolvent; these companies are allowed time and breathing space to restructure their balance sheets.
2. While under court protection, a company cannot be wound up, a receiver cannot be appointed and steps cannot be taken to

    repossess goods in the company's possession or realise debts without the consent of the examiner.

3. A limit of 100 days provides a definite timeline and structured framework that focuses the work of the examiner in formulating a rescue plan.

4. Court protection also extends to intangible assets such as intellectual property, goodwill, brands, customer lists and contracts, which are not always reflected in the company's balance sheet.

5. Examinership allows companies to repudiate onerous contracts in order to facilitate survival. This has been commonly used by multi-unit retailers paying above market value rents during recessionary years.

6. Parties who invest in a company in examinership have certainty regarding liabilities owed to creditors and a 'post-examinership' balance sheet showing the company's solvent (often debt-free) financial position.

7. If an examinership is successful, there are significant savings for the State through dividends paid to the Revenue Commissioners and maintained employment rather than redundancies paid for by the taxpayer.

8. Some negative aspects of examinership are that creditors have argued that the examinership process impinges on their statutory rights, professional costs of the process and, in some cases, dividends to creditors being low.

4.

Suitable and Unsuitable Candidates for Examinership

- Suitable Candidates for Examinership

- Examples of Suitable Candidates and Successful Examinerships

- Factors That Do *Not* Preclude a Company from Going into Examinership

- Unsuitable Candidates for Examinership

- Key Points: Suitable and Unsuitable Candidates for Examinership

Suitable Candidates for Examinership

There are a number of tests to be considered in assessing whether a company is a suitable candidate to seek to have an examiner appointed. The primary tests applied by the courts when considering whether a company can go into examinership are that:

1. it must either be unable to pay its debts or is likely to be unable to pay its debts; and
2. it must have a 'reasonable prospect of survival' as a going concern.

Inability to Pay Debts

Examinership is only available to insolvent companies. The court may appoint an examiner to the company, where it is demonstrated to the satisfaction of the court that:

- the company is, or likely to be, unable to pay its debts (based on either a balance sheet or cash-flow test);
- no company resolution or court order has been made for the winding up of the company; and
- it has a reasonable prospect of survival.

Generally, it is rarely in dispute whether a company petitioning for examinership is insolvent or not. Technically, a company is deemed to meet the above criteria if it is unable to pay its debts as they fall due (the cash-flow test) or if the value of its assets is less than the amount of its liabilities (the balance sheet test). It is important to note that in the unusual eventuality of a creditor's petition, the onus rests with the petitioner to prove that the company cannot pay its debts and it is often difficult for a creditor that does not have full access to the books and records of the company to prove this.

Reasonable Prospect of Survival

In order to succeed in getting a company into examinership, the company petitioning for court protection must prove to the court that there is a reasonable prospect of survival, i.e. that it can emerge successfully from the examinership process and continue to trade as a going concern. Thus, the court will consider, based on the information to hand, whether the company has a reasonable prospect of survival. The court will determine this by establishing to its satisfaction whether the company can operate in 'going concern', either in part or in whole if a scheme of arrangement is entered into. A key purpose of the independent expert's report (IER), which is discussed in detail in the next chapter, is to consider and present the main facts for determining whether the company has a reasonable prospect of survival.

The original legal test for considering whether a company has a prospect of survival is summarised in the pragmatic early comments of Mr Justice Gerard Lardner in the 1993 case of *Atlantic Magnetics*:

> "It seems to me that the standard is this: does the evidence lead to the conclusion that in all the circumstances herein it seems worthwhile to order an investigation by the examiner into the company's affairs and see if it can survive, there being some reasonable prospect of survival."

In 2009, on an appeal to the Supreme Court involving the examinership of *Gallium Limited*, an investment company, Mr Justice Nial Fennelly of the Supreme Court commented as follows on the reasonable prospect of survival test:

> "The statutory requirement is to show that 'there is a reasonable prospect of survival of the company'. A petitioner does not, by getting over that threshold, acquire a right to have an order made. I still think it fair to say that the section confers a 'wide discretion' on the court, or alternatively, that the court should take account of all the circumstances. The establishment of a reasonable prospect of the survival merely triggers the power, which remains discretionary."

With regard to the importance of reasonable financial projections being included in the IER, in a 2009 case involving the *Zoe Group* of construction companies, the independent accountant's projections were deemed unreasonable by the court and the petition for examinership refused. Mr Justice Peter Kelly reminded practitioners of the importance of realistic post-examinership plans and stated the following:

> "[the] degree of optimism on the part of the independent accountant borders, if it does not actually trespass, upon the fanciful. ... I have the gravest reservations about the projections on which the independent accountant has relied in forming his opinion. They appear to me to be lacking in reality given the extraordinary collapse that has occurred and the lack of any indication of the revival of fortunes in the property market. The valuations in question are out of date and can hardly be described as truly independent. I am not satisfied that the petitioners have discharged the onus of proof of showing that there is a reasonable prospect of the survival of the companies."

The reasonable prospect of survival test has been further developed over the years.

Once it is under court protection, the company is required to ensure that any liabilities incurred during the period of examinership are paid for, generally as they fall due, based on credit terms to be agreed by the company with its creditors. An examiner may assist in this regard by interceding with supplier relationships that may have deteriorated. It is important to note that while the examiner can certify liabilities and provide an additional level of comfort regarding the payment of such certified liabilities, it is far more preferable that payments of on-going costs are discharged by the company as they fall due. This will typically require cash from trading activities, some limited credit from suppliers or funding being provided by a financial institution or related party. For the period of examinership, the company should be looking to at least trade at break even. As part of the IER, a forecast will be appended to the report to show evidence that the company is able to trade for the period of the examinership. If a deficit is forecast in the IER, evidence will need to be put before the court that this deficit can be discharged by the introduction of funds during the protection period.

In addition, advisors and business owners should consider whether the following practical characteristics are possessed by a prospective examinership candidate company in order to establish whether it has the key characteristics to survive, not only the period of examinership but into the future:

- Does it provide employment?
- Does it undertake a trade?
- Does it have valuable intangible assets?
- Is there a positive mindset among the management and staff?
- Does its management have a reputation of acting with integrity?
- Is the scale of operations sufficient?
- Does it have an outline plan to exit examinership?

Providing Employment

The preservation of employment in businesses facing difficulties, but which are otherwise viable, is a primary purpose of the examinership legislation. Companies applying for the protection of the court are not required to have a minimum number of employees, though the larger the number of employees, the stronger a candidate the company will be for court protection.

Undertaking a Trade

While there are no specific exclusions in terms of the type of business that may qualify for examinership, companies should carry out trading activities, and not merely be a holding company or property holding company without a trade, although such companies may be suitable if their affairs are *related* to a trading company which is also insolvent. However, holding companies or property companies without employees would not generally be regarded as good candidates for examinership on a stand-alone basis.

Intangible Assets

Examinership provides the most appropriate mechanism with which to protect a brand, and the goodwill attaching to it, that could otherwise be lost or damaged through a liquidation or receivership. A brand does not need to be an international marque, it just needs to be a brand recognised by the industry in which it operates. A well-known brand also puts a prospective examinership candidate in a good starting position when looking to establish the source of its trade and income during the period of protection. Other intangible assets that can be protected in an examinership include customer lists, supplier-approved certifications, franchises, patents and copyrights.

Positive Approach of Management and Staff

Highs and lows within a 100-day long examinership are inevitable and it is important that management and staff approach the process with a positive attitude, given the requirement to procure creditor support for the continuing supply of goods and services, as well as to deal with criticism from creditors in very challenging circumstances.

The personal relationships built up by management and staff with the company's creditors will prove to be key. However, companies that experience prolonged periods of financial difficultly often lose staff, and those that remain are disgruntled and consumed with addressing legacy debt issues rather than attending to the core business. In such cases, where the symptoms of 'insolvency fatigue' are clear, it is important that these are addressed early on in the examinership process by the examiner and their staff. Where management and staff have already given up, mentally and emotionally, such companies tend not to be good candidates for examinership.

Management's Reputation for Acting with Integrity

Examinership is an inclusive process for all stakeholders. It is important that existing management continues to operate the business with integrity. Ultimately, court protection under examinership is not given for 'the asking'; it is a discretionary matter for the presiding judge. Correspondence from creditors depicting incumbent management in a poor light is something on which the judge may place significant reliance. In contrast, where creditors know that directors have tried their best to run the business with integrity, and that it was matters outside of the control of management that gave rise to the difficulties experienced, they will generally support existing management.

Management who may not have acted with integrity should at the outset of the examinership give consideration to the fact that, while they may remain on as employees, they will likely be required to give up their positions as directors in order for the company to emerge from the process. Where management lack sufficient commercial probity, the issue can be overcome by strengthening the board or by a third-party investor ultimately taking executive control.

Sufficient Scale of Operations

As we have seen at the beginning of this chapter, there is no minimum scale at which a company must trade in order to qualify for the appointment of an examiner. However, it is unlikely to be practical from the perspective of the costs involved if the liabilities of the company are very low, i.e. where the financial benefit of formal restructuring is outweighed by the professional cost of the process. Companies must be operating at a scale sufficient to withstand the costs of the process and be sufficiently resourced to trade during the period of protection. There is no upper limit in terms of the scale of potential candidates.

Outline Plan to Exit Examinership

Finally, a candidate company should ideally have a plan, at least in outline, as to how it will exit examinership. While the exact details of the examinership may not yet be known, candidate companies should consider how the following requirements may be financed:
* professional costs of the process, which can be paid from investment generated;
* dividends payable to creditors;
* working capital requirements to allow the company to trade going forward.

In terms of dividends payable to creditors, the statutory test is that creditors cannot be unfairly prejudiced by the examiner's proposals. As discussed earlier in Chapter 3, this means they must fare at least as well as they would in a liquidation or receivership. So, for example, if preferential creditors would get 70% on the winding up of a company, that is the minimum level that can be provided for preferential creditors in its examinership. If required, the timing of the payment of dividends can be pushed out if they relate to specific matters, which will be decided on a case-by-case basis.

With regard to the ongoing requirement for working capital, a view or opinion on the company's reasonable prospect of survival can only be formed if it is reasonable to assume that it can survive for a period of not less than 12 months. In assessing this test, the criteria usually adopted is the provision of projections, based on certain criteria, as to whether the company can sustain trading into the future. In assessing what level of working capital is required, it is important to ensure that a company emerging from examinership is sufficiently capitalised so as not to face insolvency again in the near future.

We discuss the professional costs of the examinership process in detail in Chapter 11.

Examples of Suitable Candidates and Successful Examinerships

Since the examinership legislation was first introduced, many companies across many different sectors have successfully emerged from the process. Linking to the discussion above about the key features of suitable candidates for examinership, the table below lists some examples of these businesses, with brief synopses of each case.

CASE STUDIES

Company	Brief Synopsis
Shamrock Rovers Football Club	This League of Ireland soccer club faced a number of issues, one of which was unpaid Revenue debt. Its brand was strong and there was also the social dividend associated with the value the club had to the community, particularly to young people.

Company	Brief Synopsis
Four Star Pizza	The application for court protection in this case involved a large chain of pizza takeaway restaurants, whose brand was very recognisable. Interestingly, sales of pizza by the company went up during the examinership period.
Xtra-vision	Video rentals business Xtra-vision also had a strong brand and went through the process twice, in 1993 and again in 2011. While the company no longer exists, this is more attributable to a shift in technology and consumer preferences, rather than anything connected with the examinership. The 2011 examinership involved the repudiation of onerous contracts and the closure of loss-making stores.
Fallon & Byrne Limited	Perhaps one of the most recognisable food brands in Dublin, high-end food emporium Fallon & Byrne found itself in difficulty in December 2011 when it owed Revenue in excess of €1.4 million. It had strong levels of trade, which assisted in securing investment and also in discharging liabilities as they fell due during the examinership period.
Barna Waste	In 2013 Barna Waste was the largest waste and recycling operator in the west of Ireland, with 270 employees and over 30,000 customers. Following a sales process that had been conducted on behalf of the secured lender, the directors of Barna petitioned the court for protection of the enterprise under examinership in order to restructure the business instead of the planned pre-packed receivership, whereby unsecured creditors would receive nothing. The process involved a settlement of debts, employees agreeing to a 10% pay-cut and the company emerging from the examinership on a firm financial footing.
Regan Development Limited	Regan Development Limited, which operated the Regency Hotel in Dublin, petitioned for court protection following the appointment of a receiver. The receiver was appointed on a Friday afternoon and the company came under the protection of the court on Saturday evening. The examinership allowed the McGettigan family, shareholders of Regan Development, to refinance a series of assets and to raise funding sufficient to allow all debts to be discharged in full.

Company	Brief Synopsis
McEvoy Family Foods	An examiner was appointed to McEvoy Family Foods Limited in 2012. This company had a strong media profile, having featured on the Irish version of *Dragons' Den* and winning awards such as the Ulster Bank Business Achievers Awards Best Start Up Business (Munster) in 2009. High establishment costs, delays in contract commencement and bad debts had left the company in financial difficulty in the summer of 2012. The examiner secured investment from an established brand in the agri-food sector while allowing the directors to continue to manage the company they had built up.
Bestseller	The Bestseller group of companies operates a well-established retail clothing business, trading as Vera Moda, Only, Jack & Jones and Name It. The group entered examinership in 2010, allowing it to overcome challenging trading conditions, rising retail rents and issues arising from unprofitable stores. The group streamlined its operation in Ireland and secured renewed investment. The examiner was granted the powers of a liquidator to repudiate onerous contracts by order of the court.
Atlantic Homecare	Atlantic Homecare is an established DIY brand, part of the Grafton group of companies. The company sought the protection of examinership in 2012 and continues to trade today. Issues resolved in this case included the repudiation of three restrictive leases and addressing the fixed costs associated with a downturn in trade. Investment was secured and the company recovered.
Eircom	When it sought to enter the examinership process in 2012, the Eircom Group had significant historical debts and inefficiencies, in part due to previous state ownership and repeated subsequent shareholder takeovers. Through extensive debt restructuring and a voluntary redundancy programme, the telecommunications group survived as a going concern. Now trading as Eir, this group continues to be of strategic importance in the supply of communications services in Ireland.

Company	Brief Synopsis
Brinkhall	A total of 71 jobs were saved in the Brinkhall Group of companies, which operated petrol stations in County Kildare, when it was placed into examinership in 2012. Through negotiations, debt was restructured, the supply chain with creditors was maintained, and efficiencies were gained through the retention and expertise of management.
Neylons Maintenance Services	An examiner was appointed to Neylons Maintenance Services Limited in 2012. The company found itself facing insolvency post recession, despite being the largest Irish provider of professional cleaning and maintenance services to hospitals, with a strong client list including public sector organisations.
Debenhams	Well-known department store chain Debenhams Retail (Ireland) Limited exited examinership in May 2016. Under the terms of the scheme of arrangement, the retailer's 11 stores remained open. The vast majority of its 1,400 staff were retained in addition to some 500 concession staff and 300 cosmetic staff. The company sought examinership as a result of consistent losses sustained since the start of the economic recession in 2007, excessive rents and the withdrawal of financial support from its parent company in the UK. It had owed its parent company €46 million and losses had been incurred of €22.6 million in the preceding three years. Despite emerging successfully in 2016, regrettably the company went into liquidation during the pandemic crisis in 2020.

Factors That Do *Not* Preclude a Company from Going into Examinership

The following are important to note as factors that do **not** preclude a company from entering the examinership process.

Where a Receiver Has Been Appointed (for Less Than Three Days)

While the appointment of a receiver does not necessarily preclude a company from successfully applying for examinership, it does, however, require urgent action on the part of the directors to seek professional advice and engage an independent expert to prepare an IER within three days (within 30 days in Cyprus).

Where a Provisional Liquidator Has Been Appointed

The appointment of a provisional liquidator does not preclude a company from successfully applying for examinership. In fact, it is possible for the provisional liquidation process to morph into an examinership if the presiding judge is satisfied regarding the company's reasonable prospect of survival.

Insolvency as a Result of a Once-Off Event

When a company is in difficulty or faces insolvency it is often due to a combination of factors. However, and at the same time, the fact that insolvency is caused by a single, once-off issue, problem or event does not preclude a company from availing of examinership. Examples of such issues and events can include:

- an onerous contract or lease that causes the company to lose money, as discussed in Chapter 2;
- for a retailer, a loss-making store that is draining financial resources from the rest of the business;
- a loss-making arm of a business, which, again, is dragging down other parts;
- bad debts suffered unexpectedly;
- loss of a significant customer or customers;
- downturn in trade without an appropriate 'right-sizing' of overheads to reflect same.

Unsuitable Candidates for Examinership

Examinership has provided a means for over a thousand companies to survive since the legislation was first introduced in 1990. During that time a diverse range of companies have availed of the breathing space afforded by the process to restructure, refinance, survive and then go on to thrive.

Examinership can overcome a diverse range of challenges and a binding scheme of arrangement with court authority is a powerful resolution mechanism for issues threatening the survival of a company. However, it is important for practitioners to understand that not every company can be saved and the IER stage of the petitioning process should weed out those companies that are unsuitable candidates for court protection. In fact, as we shall see in the next chapter, it was for this very reason that the IER process was introduced by the Companies (Amendment) Act 1999.

There are certain companies for which, regardless of how hard an examiner and their team may try, any restructuring process is doomed to fail. Such companies are inherently unsuitable candidates for examinership and can be divided into six distinct groups, i.e. those:
- without a reasonable prospect of survival;
- with very few or no employees;
- that are not yet trading;
- that have no means of funding a scheme of arrangement with creditors;
- where the directors and/or key management lack integrity;
- where a receiver has been appointed (for more than three days in Ireland, more than 30 days in Cyprus).

Companies Without a Reasonable Prospect of Survival

The challenges facing an insolvent company may be insurmountable. Perhaps the fundamental business concept has proven intrinsically unprofitable and there will never be enough customers at the right gross-profit margin to pay for the overheads of the business. A business may be in the wrong location, or be selling the wrong products, or have the wrong mix of key staff. A new competitor, perhaps with deep pockets, can come in to a marketplace and render the incumbent insolvent. This is a normal part of commerce. One way or the other there will always be a percentage of businesses that find themselves 'terminally' insolvent and that have no prospect of survival.

The only practical and responsible response for a company director or directors that run a terminally insolvent business is for the company to be wound up. This can be done either by way of a creditors' voluntary liquidation or through a court application for a compulsory liquidation. Directors' duties shift when a company is terminally insolvent, from the shareholders of the business to its creditors. It is not necessary for the shutters to immediately be pulled down on the business; it is reasonable for the director(s) to take some time to seek advice regarding the viable options, if any, available to the company before calling in the liquidators. This concept was tested in the *Hefferon Kearns Limited* case in 1993 when the directors of a Dublin-based construction company in examinership successfully resisted a reckless trading action against them for continuing to trade while insolvent, as options were being assessed to save the company.

Perhaps the best source of examples of companies lacking a 'reasonable prospect of survival' are the insolvent property companies in Ireland in the years following 2008 and in Cyprus from 2015. Former household names in the commercial property sector such as *Zoe Group* (2009), *McInerney Homes* (2011), *Laragan* (2009) and *Fleming Group* (2010) in Ireland, and *P. Kimonas Developments Limited* (2018) and *Hadjiyiannis* (2015) in Cyprus, were all companies that ultimately could not successfully navigate the examinership process. In the case of *McInerney Homes*, the examiner's scheme was rejected by the Supreme Court by a 3/2 majority.

Other trading companies have occasionally failed in their petitions for examinership. For example, in 2011 the *Marie Group* of Dublin convenience stores petitioned to appoint an examiner. Dismissing the petition, Mr Justice Peter Kelly noted that the company was "swimming in a sea of red ink" and would not accept that the supporting IER was backed up by an objective appraisal of the evidence, defined as critical by Mr Justice O'Donnell in the 2011 Supreme Court decision in *McInerney Homes*.

Nevertheless, it is important to note that the vast majority of petitions for examinership continue to be successful, particularly since the IER process was introduced in 1999.

Companies with Few or No Employees

As made clear by Mr Chief Justice Frank Clarke in the *Traffic Group Limited* case (see Chapter 1), the focus of examinership is to rescue otherwise viable enterprises from closure and thereby save jobs for the benefit of the community. This has been reiterated in many cases since the legislation was introduced. It is the main reason that creditors' normal contractual legal rights are suspended for a relatively short period under court protection while the company is given a second chance to restructure its affairs.

Therefore, a critical first step in examining whether a company is a suitable candidate for examinership is to assess the number of jobs at stake in the enterprise that would be threatened by its closure. Examples of successful petitions for examinership by companies supporting little or no employment are very rare, especially in recent years. However, the cases of *Skynet Airlines Limited* in 2005, *Lullymore Developments Limited* in 2008 and *Tuskar Commercial Properties Limited* in 2009 have indicated that, in very exceptional circumstances, an examinership scheme can proceed without significant employment at stake.

Companies Not Yet Trading

As we have seen, the fundamental test for examinership is the 'reasonable prospect of survival'. In practical terms, it is difficult, if not impossible, for a company to demonstrate its reasonable prospect of survival to an independent expert if it has yet to commence in business, i.e. has no track record whatsoever of trading.

However, again we find that there are exceptions to the general principle. The *Frontier Entertainment Limited* examinership scheme in 2018 allowed for the restructuring of a company whose undertaking was an entertainment venue (The Vaults) in the centre of Dublin following a bitter shareholder dispute and before it had commenced trading at all.

Companies That Have No Means of Funding a Scheme of Arrangement with Creditors

Every examinership requires a fund to facilitate a scheme of arrangement with creditors (see Chapter 9). Although dividends to creditors have been as low as 1 to 2% for unsecured creditors in certain examinership schemes, there still needs to be a fund to pay these dividends and the costs of the examinership, as well as ensuring that the company has sufficient working capital to be able to trade going forward.

Typically, the four methods of funding a scheme of arrangement are as follows:
* new equity investment;
* fresh borrowing or refinancing;
* the sale of non-core assets;
* a trading surplus at a particularly busy time of year (e.g. Christmas for a retailer).

Schemes of arrangement can be funded by alternative means, however; for example, in 2010 the truck-building company *Tony Gray & Sons Limited* funded a successful examinership scheme by ring-fencing the proceeds of an insurance claim following a devastating fire at its premises.

Regrettably, certain companies will find that they are simply unable to secure the funds to facilitate a scheme of arrangement with creditors through any of the four methods listed above. In practical terms, the availability of the necessary funding should be assessed carefully before time and effort goes into an examinership process. Clearly, any company can be rescued if a large enough equity investment is secured. The job of the professional advisor, and indeed the independent expert, is to assess the probability of securing such an investment, considering any evidence from the company in this regard, before arriving at an opinion regarding the company's reasonable prospect of survival. Many business owners, especially of family businesses, may be unreasonably optimistic about how 'investible' their company really is. The advisor must bring cold commercial logic to their assessment.

Companies Where the Directors/Management Lack Integrity

Once appointed, the examiner works closely with the board of directors to help steer the company through its restructuring phase. As discussed in Chapter 7, the examiner does not take over the running of the company, unless in very exceptional circumstances. Instead, the examiner has the power to convene, set the agenda for and preside over company board meetings, although he or she does not vote at those meetings. Effectively, the role of the examiner at board meetings has been likened to the role of a strong non-executive chair. In the vast majority of examinerships, the company continues under the stewardship of its directors.

In some examinership cases, certain directors have been found to lack the integrity and commercial probity that are critical for a scheme of arrangement to be successful. If directors deliberately treat creditors poorly, especially if they are dishonest, the support of creditors will likely not be forthcoming. Furthermore, directors who enter the examinership process for personal gain are unlikely to remain focused on the *company's* success throughout the restructuring phase.

Clearly, examinership is not a process designed to give cover to directors who wish to arrange affairs to suit their own ends. While this sort of abuse of the process is rare, it is important that examiners remain vigilant in their monitoring of the company to ensure that directors, sometimes under massive personal pressure, do not lose sight of their obligations under company law.

Companies Where a Receiver Has Been Appointed for More than Three Days in Ireland or 30 Days in Cyprus

Among the most vociferous opponents of examinership are the secured creditors communities in both Ireland and Cyprus where their normally unassailable rights to appoint a receiver under a fixed or floating charge can be challenged with an examinership petition.

The usual enforcement option for a secured creditor of a trading company is to appoint a receiver to receive the assets of the company and either trade them or realise them in whatever way the receiver sees fit. Invariably, the result of a receivership is the ultimate liquidation of the remaining insolvent company shell when its assets are sold. Occasionally, a receivership may rescue some or all of the jobs in the business; however, a receiver is under no obligation to seek to preserve employment in a company. The receiver is a creature of the secured creditor's charge document; in practical terms, therefore, the receiver's master is the secured creditor (usually a bank) who will seek the maximum return from the loan.

The introduction of examinership changed the usual dynamic of secured creditor enforcement because it meant that if a borrower or debtor company was sufficiently organised it could apply instead for court protection rather than enter receivership and liquidation. The difference between the time afforded in Ireland and Cyprus is striking; three days in Ireland compared to a generous 30 days in Cyprus.

The three-day time limit means it is difficult for an insolvent company to have an IER and petition prepared in time, though it is by no means impossible. Though the three-day period does not include weekend days or public holidays, it is critical to note that the day the receiver is appointed counts as Day 1. Therefore, for example, if a company goes into receivership on a Monday evening, the examinership petition must take place by Wednesday evening at the very latest, which means the time available to the petitioner is only two days in practical terms.

The time constraints mean that if a company only starts considering the examinership option after a receiver has been appointed, the task becomes more and more difficult as the clock ticks down. Once the time has expired, the company can no longer avail of the examinership option and is no longer a candidate for the process.

Key Points: Suitable and Unsuitable Candidates for Examinership

1. For the court to place a company into examinership, it must be unable to pay its debts and it must have a reasonable prospect of survival as a going concern.
2. A company is deemed unable to pay its debts if the value of its assets are less than the amount of its liabilities, and if a creditor who is indebted by at least €20,000 has issued a service of demand to pay the sum and the company has neglected to do so.
3. The court will review an independent expert's report (IER) and financial projections to determine whether the company can emerge successfully from the examinership process and continue to trade as a going concern.
4. Companies should ideally have employees outside of the directors' immediate families whose livelihoods are dependent upon the survival of the business.
5. Holding companies that do not trade are not generally regarded as good candidates for examinership, unless their affairs are related to a trading company which is also insolvent.
6. Strong brand recognition puts a company in a good starting position when looking to establish trade and income during the protection period. The brand also allows a potential investor to understand the company's perceived value, which provides more certainty in terms of what they are investing in.
7. Executive management teams who have already given up tend not to be good candidates for the ups and downs of a 100-day long examinership process. It is also important that they act with integrity and build strong relationships with creditors.
8. A company cannot enter examinership if a receiver has been appointed for more than three days (30 days in Cyprus).

5.

The Appointment of an Examiner

- Introduction
- The Examiner
- The Independent Expert's Report
- Application for the Protection of the Court
- Key Points: The Appointment of an Examiner

Introduction

This chapter discusses in detail the process for appointing an examiner, setting out who can be an examiner, who can be an independent expert and what is required from the independent expert's report (IER). The IER has been the lynchpin of the petition process since the requirement was introduced by the Companies (Amendment) (No. 2) Act 1999 that a company should demonstrate that it has a 'reasonable prospect of survival' before it can qualify for examinership. The chapter also describes the detailed legal documentation required to petition the court, how the petitioner can navigate the process and what happens at the court hearings as the process begins.

The Examiner

An examiner is the person, usually an accountant and/or a licensed insolvency practitioner[1] with experience in the field of restructurings and insolvencies, appointed by the court to act as examiner to a company seeking protection. The application to appoint an examiner will be accompanied by a 'consent to act' presented to the court by the nominated examiner together with an affidavit of fitness, usually from a solicitor confirming that the nominated examiner is fit to act as an interim examiner and/or examiner. These documents form part of the petition papers (which are discussed later in this chapter).

The main functions of the examiner are to examine the affairs of the company, oversee the formulation, acceptance and implementation of proposals for a compromise of debts owed to creditors, or scheme of arrangement put to the members and creditors of the company, and to facilitate the company's emergence from the examinership process. (The role of the examiner and its various functions are explained in more detail in Chapter 7.)

It is important to note that the examiner acts independently of the company's directors, shareholders, creditors or its prospective investors.

---

[1] In accordance with section 633 of the Companies Act 2014, to be a corporate insolvency practitioner in Ireland you must hold a practising certificate issued either by an IAASA (the Irish Auditing and Accounting Supervisory Authority) regulated professional accountancy body or the Law Society of Ireland. Other "persons of practical experience" may also be authorised to act directly by IAASA.

In this regard, the examiner takes on a number of roles during the course of the examinership:

- as chairperson, in monitoring the operations of the company and the formulation of proposals;
- as corporate finance advisor in assisting the company in procuring investment;
- as mediator in dealing with the disputes that invariably arise with aggrieved creditors; and
- as an officer of the court that appointed them, to which they must ultimately report.

It is often explained to the stakeholders of a company in examinership that the role of the examiner is similar to that of a non-executive chairperson. For example, the examiner has the statutory right to set the agenda for and attend board meetings, though he or she does not vote at these. In addition, the examiner does not take over executive functions of the company in examinership unless these functions are vested in the examiner by the court. (This happens in certain circumstances, which are discussed in Chapter 7.)

In Ireland, the qualifications required in order to act as examiner are set out in the Companies Act 2014, which states that "a person is not qualified to be appointed or act as an examiner of a company unless he or she would be qualified to act as its liquidator". In order to be appointed as a liquidator to a company in accordance with the Companies Act 2014, a nominee must be a licensed and insured insolvency practitioner as set out above.

In practice, the examiner is invariably the insolvency partner of an accountancy firm.

Cyprus

The legislation in Cyprus is similar to that in Ireland; the examiner of a company must be qualified to act as an advisor according to the provisions of the Insolvency Practitioners Law of 2015 and be a licensed insolvency practitioner. In order to obtain an insolvency practitioner's licence, the person concerned must be a member of one of the following associations:

- the Insolvency Service of Cyprus;
- the Institute of Certified Public Accountants of Cyprus (ICPAC); or
- the Pan-Cyprus Bar Association.

While not expressly set out in the Cypriot legislation, it is a pre-requisite for any nominated examiner to be independent from the company, its directors and shareholders, and hold the interests of all stakeholders in equal proportion. As set out above, the examiner is an officer of the court and must act fairly and independently of the company and the interests of its promoters or any one class of creditor. In the 2018 Cypriot case of *P. Kimonas Developments Limited*, a property development company located in Nicosia, it was contended by the secured creditors of the company in their submissions to the court that the nominated examiner was not independent and therefore would not treat the interests of all stakeholders equally. In this case, the nominated examiner was the company's advisor, who had previously undertaken a valuation of the company's properties; he was also the independent expert who prepared the IER to accompany the company's petition for examinership. Ultimately, the petition did not proceed as it was withdrawn by the company.

As discussed later in this chapter, except in exceptional circumstances, the petition for court protection must be accompanied by an independent expert's report. The independent expert will be either the auditor of the company or a qualified accountant or auditor who is independent of the company. The question of whether the independent expert should subsequently act as examiner to the company has been the subject of a number of decisions in the Irish courts. In a 2001 case involving *Tuskar Resources Plc*, an oil exploration company, the presiding judge ruled that there was no statutory restriction on the court appointing the independent accountant (now known as the independent expert) as examiner to the company, although it was noted that there may be cases where it would be inappropriate to do so. In 2005, the issue of the independent expert acting as examiner was again considered in the case of *Skynet Airlines Limited*, in which the court indicated that there was some merit in allowing such an appointment, as there would be a considerable saving in costs if only one accountant had to investigate the company's prospects of survival.

This approach was followed in the same year by the court in a decision involving *EU-Jetops Limited*, a Shannon-based, low-fares airline, and in *Lynch Freight (Kilmallock) Limited* in 2012, in a decision handed down by Mr Justice Peter Kelly.

In the 2015 examinership of *Centre for Irish and European Security Limited*, the independent expert and nominated examiner were from the same firm of accountants. Neither the judge nor the Revenue Commissioners raised any issue with the fact that both parties were from the same firm and the court proceeded to appoint the nominated examiner.

Joint Examiners

While it is commonplace in Ireland for two practitioners to be appointed to act as either joint liquidators or joint receivers (liquidators appointed by the High Court, liquidators appointed in voluntary liquidations at a creditors' meeting, or receivers appointed by secured creditors), there has never been an appointment of joint examiners.

The idea of the appointment of joint examiners has only been presented to the court on one occasion. In the 2012 *Brinkhall Group* case, the court was asked to consider the appointment of joint examiners, the nominated examiner being unsure if he could commit the requisite amount of time to the case and being unable to commit to attending creditors' meetings due to personal circumstances. As a result, the petition requested that the court consider appointing the nominated examiner and/or another insolvency practitioner from the same firm. The petition noted that both practitioners had no conflicts of interest and consented to act as examiners, and both had affidavits of suitability sworn on their behalf by a practising solicitor who had knowledge of their previous experience and skills.

On hearing the petition, Ms Justice Mary Finlay Geoghegan was satisfied to appoint an examiner to the companies; however, she also stated that she felt it was inappropriate for joint examiners to be appointed to the company. She proceeded to appoint the originally nominated practitioner as examiner to the companies and set out that if any difficulties should arise as a result of the examiner's personal circumstances, he should come back to court and seek directions on how to proceed.

Disputes Regarding the Nominee to Act as Examiner

When seeking protection of the court, the petition presented to the court for the appointment must include the name of the person nominated to act as the examiner. While in most cases there will be no issues in relation to this, in certain circumstances some of the stakeholders in a business will take issue with the nominated examiner or the manner in which the nominated examiner is selected. An example of this was seen in the early days of the examinership in 1991 of *Presswell Limited*, a printing company and manufacturer of self-adhesive labels and tapes. In this instance, at the full hearing of the petition, a creditor objected to the appointment of the examiner because the resolution to appoint an examiner to the company had not been signed by one of the required directors, who had been out of the country. The hearing of the petition was dismissed, but the judge commented that there was nothing to stop the petitioners immediately re-presenting the petition. Once the issue in the petition had been resolved, the petition was re-presented and an examiner was duly appointed.

Something similar to this was seen in the 2012 case of *Advanced Balloon Technologies Limited*, a manufacturer of medical devices, where two of the company's four shareholders presented a petition to appoint an examiner. The two shareholders who had petitioned to put the company into examinership were based in Ireland, and the remaining two shareholders were based in the US. A dispute had arisen between the US and Irish based directors, and although neither group was opposed to the appointment of an examiner *per se*, the US shareholders objected to the individual nominated by the Irish shareholders as examiner. It therefore transpired that, at the full hearing of the petition, the judge not only had to decide on whether to appoint an examiner, but also on whom to appoint. Mr Justice Peter Kelly ruled that the examiner nominated by the majority shareholders should be appointed, with the decision largely based on the fact that the US-based majority shareholders had been deprived of their legal right, as majority shareholders, to pass the resolution to present a petition and in turn nominate an examiner.

The decision of Mr Justice Kelly in *Advanced Balloon Technologies Limited* was applied in similar circumstances in the 2018 case of *Yvolve Sports Limited*. In this case, there was a dispute between the Irish and the Taiwanese shareholders in the company. The Irish shareholders sought the appointment of an examiner following a breakdown in the relationship between the two sides. At the petition hearing, the Taiwanese shareholders nominated an alternative examiner to the one originally appointed by the Irish shareholders. In this case, Ms Justice Costello decided that the first examiner nominated by the Irish shareholders would be appointed.

It is also interesting and surprising to note that, at the time of writing, only one female examiner has been appointed (Sarah-Jane O'Keeffe of Baker Tilly in the 2019 *Eastern Seaboard Bar and Grill Limited* case), despite the fact that women now hold many key positions in companies, the public service, professional firms and the legal system. It is expected that this gender imbalance among examiners will be redressed in the coming years.

The Independent Expert's Report

As introduced in Chapter 4, an independent expert's report (IER) is a prescribed report prepared by an independent expert (typically an accountant) and submitted to the court with the rest of the documentation required for a petition for examinership. Its purpose is to outline to the court specific information in relation to the company, most importantly demonstrating that the company seeking court protection has a 'reasonable prospect of survival' to operate profitably going forward, provided that the examinership is successful. (*Note*: an IER is only written if there is a prospect for survival as the independent expert is required to verify this.) In addition, an IER must establish and demonstrate that the examinership process will yield a greater return to the company's creditors than a winding up of the company. This is done through the preparation of a statement of affairs by the independent expert (discussed in more detail below).

The IER is a critically important document for any examinership process. It is the document upon which legal counsel relies to draft the petition seeking the protection of the court. It is also the main document upon which the court must rely in order to decide whether to grant court protection. The IER provides an excellent starting point for the examiner in relation to identifying the matters to be addressed when attempting to formulate proposals to be put to the members and/or creditors of the company.

The accuracy of any IER depends on accurate information being provided by the company, which must be provided with utmost good faith. A material non-disclosure to the court by a company (or indeed subsequently by the examiner) can result in the removal of its protection. The independent expert must be satisfied that the information provided for the preparation of the IER is true and accurate and that there has not been a failure to disclose all material facts. An independent expert can be questioned by the court or by an opposing creditor; therefore, they must be in a position to stand over any aspect of the IER they have prepared.

While an IER can be prepared within a relatively short period of time, this is dependent on the availability of information required by the independent expert and the complexity of the case. The cost of an IER also varies, depending on these factors, although for an SME business it typically ranges between €2,000 and €5,000.

An IER is typically divided into a number of subsections, as follows:
- Background
- History and Business Activities
- Financial History
- Sources of Financial Difficulties
- Taxation Liabilities
- Future of the Company
- Management Team
- Reasonable Prospects of Survival – Conditions
- Ability to Trade during Examinership – Cash-flow Projections
- Scheme of Arrangement

- Statement of Affairs
- Payment of Pre-Petition Liabilities.

Background

In this initial section, the independent expert outlines the background of the company, providing commentary on the date of its incorporation, its registration number with the Companies Registration Office (CRO) and details of its registered office. The IER will also set out details of shareholdings in the company, as well as its existing directors and company secretary. Another key aspect of the IER is to outline details of company management and employment. As we have seen, examinership was first introduced in 1990 with the aim of preserving employment through the restructuring of viable businesses. It is therefore critical to outline details of the employees, including management, who rely directly on the company for their livelihoods, as well as information about the liabilities the State will incur in terms of redundancy payments to employees in the event the company ceases to trade.

History and Business Activities

The IER includes an account of the history of the company, setting out its business activities and key milestones achieved since its incorporation. The report outlines the sector(s) in which the company operates, referring to its key clients and any notable projects the company has completed in the past or is currently working on. The purpose of including such information is to highlight to the court that the company has intangible assets, such as a reputable list of clients, good relationships with suppliers, trademarks, patents, brand value, know-how among key employees, etc. Such positive indicators can assist the company in addressing the reasonable prospect of survival test.

Financial History

As we have seen, as well as demonstrating that it has a reasonable prospect of survival, the company must also showcase that it is either insolvent or about to become insolvent in order for the court to consider the examinership petition. In this regard, information surrounding the financial history of the company is critical to demonstrate that it is not currently in a position to discharge its debts as they fall due.

A company can either be balance-sheet insolvent, whereby its liabilities exceed its assets, or cash-flow insolvent. A typical example of a balance-sheet insolvency is that brought about by a loan incurred by the company, which is non-performing and is having a negative impact on a company's balance sheet. Cash-flow insolvency is typically seen in the event of slow or non-payments of creditors, which results in the company having insufficient cash flow available to discharge liabilities as they fall due.

The independent expert will prepare a table summarising the company's historical financial performance, which normally consists of the last five accounting periods. He or she will outline at a high level the trading position of the company over that period, which will usually indicate increasing losses. Where applicable, a commentary will also be provided to explain the company's poor trading results. The independent expert will also place emphasis on any encouraging signs the company has shown in recent trading figures of a reasonable prospect of its survival. For this to occur, it is very important that the company keeps accurate monthly management accounts.

It is important to note that a company may be solvent at the time of presenting a petition for examinership once it can demonstrate that circumstances will change for it in the near future. Examples of such a scenario would be a company that has just lost legal proceedings with substantial costs being made against it, or a company that has lost a key contract critical to its trade.

Sources of Financial Difficulties

The independent expert is required to outline the factors that have led to the company seeking court protection, together with details of any efforts made to address these issues prior to petitioning for examinership. The independent expert will also set out their views on how to potentially reverse those difficulties during the protection period, which will assist the company to strengthen its prospect of survival going forward. (Further commentary on the conditions of survival is provided below.)

Taxation Liabilities

More often than not, the Revenue Commissioners (Revenue) is listed as a creditor of the company and usually enjoys a super preferential and/or preferential status when it comes to formulating proposals for a compromise and scheme of arrangement. Revenue adopts an active role in the examination process, and therefore the IER is required to outline details of the monies owed to Revenue. The independent expert will also outline details of any prior instalment arrangements entered into with Revenue or discussions in relation to the settlement of historical Revenue liabilities, in addition to any notice of attachment on the company's bank account, if any. The attachment will be rescinded if the company is successful in obtaining the protection of the court.

It is essential for a company in examinership to remain fully tax compliant in relation to all post petition taxes.

Future of the Company

Arguably the most important section of an IER is the commentary about the future prospects of the company. The independent expert is required to set out the future prospects and plans for the company should it enter and successfully exit the examination process. The IER will outline details of any plans for expansion, ongoing and future projects, and opportunities within the company's sector, and will refer to any successful trading figures the company may have recorded in recent times. The independent expert will outline their views on requirements for investment to ensure that the company is a viable enterprise following the examination process and will also highlight key factors, such as the preservation of employment. The independent expert will also produce 12-month trading projections for the company, which are appended to the IER, to determine whether profitability is possible.

Management Team

The IER must also list the company's directors together with its Company Secretary and its auditor. The registered addresses for each are also required to be listed. In addition, details of any other directorships held are required to be disclosed in the IER.

It is important to note that each director of the company is responsible for ensuring that the correct information is provided to the independent expert for the preparation of their report. While the independent expert can carry out a certain amount of background checks on directors and the company, they are reliant on the directors to provide all relevant and accurate information on their directorships and the company's affairs. A failure to disclose required information can be grounds for an objection to any such application to enter examinership. A non-disclosure to the court can have the impact of placing greater scrutiny on a company and make the examinership process all the more challenging.

Reasonable Prospects of Survival – Conditions

As discussed above, the IER will outline the various difficulties that have led the company to petition for examinership and seek court protection. The independent expert is required to set out the basis, or bases, for their belief that the company will have a reasonable prospect of survival. Invariably, the independent expert's analysis that a company has a reasonable prospect of survival will entail that the company meets a number of conditions. While these conditions will vary from company to company, and from case to case, depending on the circumstances surrounding the reason it has sought the protection of the court, there are a number of ever-present conditions the company, together with its examiner, must satisfy:

- the protection of the court is granted to the company;
- the securing of investment and/or the generation of a sufficient cash surplus during the protection period which will provide sufficient capital to fund a higher dividend to the creditors of the company compared to a liquidation, and future cash-flow requirements to operate the business;
- the acceptance of an appropriate scheme of arrangement by the members and creditors of the company and its approval by the court, which may include a partial write-down of existing debts owing to the creditors.

In addition to the above ever-present conditions, other conditions typically included in an IER are:

- the settling or restructuring of any secured debt;
- the repudiation of any onerous leases or contracts; and
- the resolving of any issues faced at board level.

While these are common conditions, they are not certain to arise and each IER is prepared on a case-by-case basis. If appointed, an examiner will use these conditions as a template to prepare a roadmap for the examinership, with the ultimate aim of returning to court at the end of the process with only one condition remaining unsatisfied, i.e. the approval of the proposals by the court. If an examiner returns to the court seeking approval of the scheme of arrangement, and a number of conditions identified in the IER remain unsatisfied, this will greatly reduce the likelihood of proposals in the scheme being approved. The greater the number of conditions that remain unsatisfied, the greater the uncertainty surrounding a company's reasonable prospect of survival.

Ability to Trade during Examinership – Cash-flow Projections

Another key element of every IER is the cash-flow projections that are prepared for the company for the period it will remain under court protection. When a company is placed under the protection of the court, it tends to have a negative impact on its credit terms with suppliers, who often then require cash on delivery for the purchase of goods and materials. In order to be in a position to appoint an examiner, the court must be satisfied that the company will be able to trade and meet all debts as they fall due during the protection period. In this regard, the company will prepare 10-week cash-flow projections in order to illustrate that it will be in a position to continue to trade if the court were to grant it protection.

The independent expert must also be satisfied that the company's projections are realistic and achievable before putting them before the court for consideration. These projections are also of significant importance to the examiner for a number of reasons. The examiner is required to monitor the company's cash flow during the protection period in order to ensure the company has the ability to trade. The examiner will investigate any material differences between the company's projected and actual cash-flow positions and will also report regularly to the court on the company's trade during the protection period. The examiner, as an officer of the court, has a duty to return to court as soon as he or she forms a view that the company cannot continue to trade or has no reasonable prospect of survival. If a company cannot explain any material discrepancies in respect of its cash-flow position during the protection period, the examiner is required to bring this to the attention of the court, together with a view as to whether the company should continue to trade.

The examiner can also use the cash-flow projections as a negotiating tool with key suppliers to the company. Once a company is under protection of the court, a stop is placed on the payment of any monies owing to its creditors as at the date of the petition. This can equate to significant sums of money owing to key suppliers in certain instances and they may, as a result, be reluctant to continue to supply the company going forward. An examiner can use the cash-flow projections to demonstrate to any key suppliers that the company will be in a position to discharge any sums due in respect of goods or services provided during the protection period, though probably on stricter credit terms or even on a cash-on-delivery basis. The loss of key suppliers can have a detrimental impact on a business's ability to trade while under protection of the court; therefore, the preparation of realistic cash-flow projections can greatly assist it in retaining the support of its key suppliers.

Statement of Affairs

As discussed above, one of the purposes of the IER is to demonstrate
to the court and to the creditors of the company that they, along with
the employees, would fare better following an examinership process
as opposed to a winding-up scenario. For the creditors of the company,
the benefit of an examinership is the prospect of the company protecting its core business and goodwill, thereby providing a sound platform for the examiner to maximise the funds available for a scheme
of arrangement so that creditors can receive the maximum possible
percentage of the debts they are owed. This key point is demonstrated
by a statement of affairs customarily appended to the IER.

The statement of affairs lists details of the company's assets and liabilities and compares the position of the company as a going concern, i.e.
operating indefinitely, if an examinership is successful and in a winding
up scenario if the company is liquidated. In a winding up, the level of
deficit tends to be far greater than in a going-concern scenario; this is
attributable to the reduction in a company's realisable assets in a winding up scenario and the increase in preferential creditors as a result of
redundancies. An example of a statement of affairs as typically prepared
for an IER is provided below.

EXAMPLE 5.1: STATEMENT OF AFFAIRS

ABC Limited

Estimated Statement of Affairs

	Going Concern €	Wind Up €
Encumbered Assets		
Property	675,000	100,000
Fixed Charge Creditor (Owed €800k)	–675,000	–100,000
	0	0

Unencumbered Assets

Fixtures and Fittings	45,000	9,000
Motor Vehicles	27,500	9,075
Stocks	250,000	85,000
Cash & Floats	5,000	5,000
Prepayments	100,000	0
Funds Available to Preferential Creditors	**440,250**	**105,575**
Preferential Creditors		
Revenue Commissioners	–65,000	–65,000
Rates	–25,000	–25,000
Employees – Minimum Notice, Arrears of Wages & Holiday Pay		–150,000
Total Preferential Creditors	–90,000	–240,000
Funds Available for Floating Charge Creditor	**350,250**	**–134,425**
Floating Charge Creditor		
Bank	–125,000	–700,000
Funds Available for Unsecured Creditors	**225,250**	**–834,425**
Unsecured Creditors		
Unsecured Creditors	–850,000	–850,000
Bank Overdraft	–15,000	–15,000
Revenue Commissioners	–25,000	–25,000
Directors Loans	–250,000	–250,000
Accruals	–75,500	–75,500
Total Unsecured Creditors	**–1,215,500**	**–1,215,500**
Overall Deficit	**–990,250**	**–2,049,925**

Note: the statement of affairs also reflects details of any security held by a secured creditor. This is critically important to show as it can have a material impact of the availability of funds to the various classes of creditors in a winding up.

In the above example, the secured creditor has a fixed and floating charge. When there is a deficit of a return to the secured creditor in respect of the fixed security held, this deficit is then subject to a floating charge, which ranks above the unsecured creditors of a company. The statement of affairs lists the funds available to the various classes of creditors and provides a guideline or estimate for the level of dividend that would be payable to each class of creditor in a winding-up scenario. This is important because the examiner must take this 'waterfall' into consideration when deciding whether or not they are in a position to formulate a scheme of arrangement to put to the members and creditors of the company. A key factor for the examiner to consider is whether a creditor is unfairly prejudiced in any of the proposals formulated. A creditor cannot fare any worse off under proposals following compromises on debts owed than they would in a winding up. For example, the above statement of affairs clearly indicates that the unsecured creditors will not receive any dividend in a winding up as there is a deficit of €834,425 before their claims are considered.

Payment of Pre-Petition Liabilities

As we have seen, a condition of an examinership process is placing a stop on the payment of all monies due to the company's creditors as at the date of the petition. However, the independent expert can recommend in their report that certain pre-petition liabilities are discharged as they are essential to the continued running of the business. The pre-petition liabilities that are recommended to be discharged will vary from case to case, depending on the industry and sector in which the petitioning company operates. That said, however, the following liabilities would typically be recommended for payment:
* wages;
* insurance; and
* merchant service charges.

Discharging payments of pre-petition liabilities is quite common in construction industry examinerships. As part of preparing the IER, the independent expert will discuss and review the current contracts of the company with its directors. The independent expert will identify key suppliers and pre-petition invoices that will be required to be paid in order to ensure the company has a reasonable prospect of survival. For example, if a warranty or certificate is required from a materials supplier in order to allow an architect to sign off on payment to the company, then the independent expert will recommend that this invoice is included in the list of pre-petition payments to be made.

The independent expert may also state that certain additional pre-petition liabilities may need to be discharged during the examinership process that have not been identified at the time of preparation of the IER. However, it is important to note that this is not a common occurrence and it is at the discretion of the examiner whether or not to make an application to the court seeking approval to discharge pre-petition liabilities. Incurring higher costs, the examiner must be satisfied that failure to discharge the liabilities concerned will result in the company not being in a position to continue to trade.

Application for the Protection of the Court

Circuit Court Jurisdiction

Petitions to appoint an examiner are generally brought to the High Court; however, there are provisions within the legislation allowing for such a petition to be brought to the Circuit Court.

In order to file a petition with the Circuit Court to appoint an examiner, the company must meet two of the three criteria as defined by the Companies Act 2014, and subsequently amended by the Companies (Accounting) Act 2017:
- balance sheet does not exceed €6 million;
- annual turnover does not exceed €12 million;
- number of employees does not exceed 50.

The appropriate Circuit Court is located in the region, or 'circuit', in which:
1. the company has its registered office at the time of presenting the petition; or
2. where the company has its principal place of business.

In the 2017 case of *Com-Plas Packaging Limited and Scriptdale Trading Limited,* although the legal team and notice parties were all based in Dublin, the case was remitted to the Eastern Circuit as the company's registered office was in Naas, County Kildare.

In the case of a company seeking protection from the Circuit Court, an originating notice of motion, rather than a petition, will be brought:

1. in the county in which the company has its registered office, or principal place of business, at the time of the presentation of the originating notice of motion; or
2. if, at that time, there is no registered office of the company or society, and its principal place of business is outside the State, in the Dublin Circuit.

It is required that the originating notice of motion is verified by an affidavit sworn by, or on behalf of, the party making the application. The Circuit Court rules state that: "On the same day as the originating notice of motion is presented, or as soon as possible thereafter, the applicant shall apply *ex parte* to the court for directions as to the proceedings to be taken on the originating notice of motion".[2]

On hearing the application, which may or not be heard on presentation, the court may make an order and give directions in line with the following:

- give directions as to the parties on whom the originating notice of motion should be served, the mode of service and the time for such service;
- give directions as to the manner in which creditors of the company are to be notified or may be notified of their right to be heard at the hearing of the originating notice of motion;
- fix a date for the hearing of the originating notice of motion as this hearing will decide on the appointment of the examiner;
- give directions as to whether the originating notice of motion should be advertised and, if so, how;
- where appropriate, place the company under the protection of the court for such a period the court thinks necessary in order to allow for the submission of an IER (applies in cases where court protection is urgently required but no IER accompanied the application);
- where appropriate, make an order appointing a proposed examiner on an interim basis until the date fixed for the hearing of the originating notice of motion.

Centre of Main Interests

As many companies are now operating internationally, it is important to determine a company's 'centre of main interests' (COMI) when considering where to undertake insolvency proceedings. EU law states that the COMI should correspond to the place where the enterprise conducts

---

[2] Circuit Court Rules (Companies Act 2014) 2015 (S.I. No. 471 of 2015).

the administration of its interests on a regular basis and is therefore ascertainable by other parties. On this basis, cross-border insolvency proceedings should be taken in the EU Member State (with the exception of Denmark) where the debtor has its 'centre of main interest'. The following questions should be asked in determining a debtor's COMI:

- Who has control over the company?
- Where are the majority of its employees based?
- Where is the head office?
- Where is the administrative support based?
- Where is the management team and finance function based?
- Where are the sales and orders generated from?

It is important to note that where a company has commenced insolvency proceedings in another EU Member State then a second examinership proceeding cannot be commenced in Ireland. The issue of COMI arose in the petition for the *FCR Media Limited* (the company behind Golden Pages) examinership in 2017. The protection of the court was sought for two companies, one with a registered address in Ireland and the other with a registered address in Lithuania. The Lithuanian company held and owned the intellectual property in respect of the Irish company; therefore it was also necessary to seek court protection for the Lithuanian company. The company's lawyers argued that the Lithuanian company's COMI was Ireland on the basis that the Lithuanian company was controlled and managed from Ireland.

Who Can Present a Petition for Examinership?

A petition can be presented to the court by the following parties:

- the company;
- the director(s) of the company (if a company has more than two directors, this can be the majority of the directors);
- the member(s) of the company holding shares at the date of the presentation of the petition. (If members are making the petition, they must hold no less than 10% of the paid-up shares, carrying 10% of the voting rights.);
- the creditors of the company; or
- a combination of any of the above parties.

In practice, it is rare for the creditors of a company to have sufficient information about its affairs to successfully petition to have an examiner appointed, though this has occurred in a handful of cases over the years, notably in the 2009 case of *Golden Discs Limited*, a music and entertainment retailer, where Sony Music made the examinership application. In another case, in 2014, involving Cork-based property group *O'Flynn*

Construction Company and its related companies, a petition to have an examiner appointed was presented by the companies' creditor Carbon Finance Limited, which acquired the interest of cross-guaranteed loans between the companies and the National Asset Management Agency (NAMA). The *O'Flynn* case was ultimately dismissed as it was deemed an abuse of process by the American fund that launched the petition.

It is important to consider that the party taking the petition, either individually or collectively, will bear the costs associated with taking the petition.

Preparing a Petition without an IER

Where a petition is presented without an IER, the court may be satisfied to proceed if, by reason of exceptional circumstances outside the control of the petitioner, the IER is not available in time to accompany the petition. This occurred in the *Golden Discs* case (see above) where the petitioner, Sony Music, did not have access to the company's books and records, and therefore was unable to include an independent accountant's report (now known as an IER) as part of its petition papers. The court appointed an interim examiner and made an order for the nominated independent accountant to prepare their report prior to the hearing of the petition. In such instances, the court may place the company under the protection of the court until such time that an IER can be provided to determine the prospect for the company's survival. The court would normally allow no more than 10 days within which to submit the IER. (*Note*: it has been determined that where a receiver has been appointed, this does not fall within the category of an exceptional circumstance.) If a report is not submitted within the timeframe set out by the court, the company will cease to be under its protection.

Preparing the Petition Paperwork

The petition for examinership is presented on an *ex-parte* basis, meaning that the application is brought by one party, in the absence of notification to other parties, and the court will rely heavily on the petition being accurate and that it is made in the utmost good faith. Failure to disclose any available information that is material to the examination process and/or failure to exercise the utmost good faith in the preparation of the petition paperwork, may lead the court to decline to continue hearing the petition. Therefore, it is essential to avoid any errors or omissions in the petition paperwork.

Every petition for the appointment of an examiner must be verified by a grounding affidavit to support the application to court. The petition paperwork will typically comprise the following:

1. A grounding affidavit containing:
   (a) The petition for examinership (in the Circuit Court, an originating notice of motion), to include basic information, such as:
      - the full name and address of the petitioner;
      - the date of incorporation of the company;
      - the registered office of the company;
      - the nominal and paid-up share capital of the company;
      - the objects and main business of the company;
      - that the company cannot or is likely to be unable to pay its debts;
      - that no resolution subsists for the winding up of the company;
      - that no order has been made for the winding up of the company.
   (b) the independent expert's report (IER);
   (c) any proposals for a scheme of arrangement (if these have been prepared to be presented to interested parties); and
   (d) a letter of consent from the nominated examiner confirming their consent to act as interim examiner/examiner.
2. An affidavit of fitness from a person, usually a solicitor, who knows the nominated examiner and their skillset in relation to examinerships.
3. An affidavit of compliance sworn by the nominated examiner that they meet the requirements of the Companies Act 2014.

The petition should be presented at the relevant court's central office, where directions will be given to the petitioner regarding the time and place that the assigned judge will hear the petition. This invariably takes place that same day. Once the petition is lodged with the court, the CRO must be notified within three days.

Interim Examiners

On hearing the *ex-parte* application, the court may give orders and directions as it thinks fit. These directions may include whom the petition should be served upon (i.e. the most important creditors, to whom an actual copy of the full petition papers should be sent), the mode of service, the time for such service, the date for the hearing of the petition and whether the petition should be advertised and if so, how. If the court deems there is sufficient urgency to warrant it, it may appoint an examiner on an interim basis. An interim examiner will have the same powers and duties as a fully appointed examiner.

There must be good reason for an interim examiner to be appointed, and an interim examiner may not be necessary in every case. For example, in the 2018 case of *Yvolve Sports Limited*, an interim examiner was necessary to allow shareholders to start communicating and the interim examiner called a board meeting to enable this. In the 2019 case of *M.D.Y. Construction Limited* ('M.D.Y.'), an interim examiner was necessary to negotiate with both the county councils involved and with subcontractors, as construction work had ceased on all sites, including those where social housing was being built. In addition, the interim examiner was able to meet with the receiver in respect of a claim by NAMA and to get started on the investment process immediately in order to keep the existing contracts. Otherwise, the company would likely have folded.

In the event an interim examiner has been appointed and is due back in court for the full hearing of the petition, they must submit a report of the work they have undertaken during the period of this appointment. It is essential that the interim examiner keep and maintain a true record of all liabilities certified by them pursuant to the Companies Act 2014 and provide a full report on the certified liabilities to the court.

Related Companies

It is possible for an examiner to be appointed over a group of related companies. Again, the same provisions apply as to the court's orders and directions. An application for the appointment of an examiner of a related company shall, if brought by any person other than the petitioner or the examiner of the original company, be brought by way of notice of motion served upon the examiner and petitioner. The moving party to the application must verify that, to their knowledge, there are no other insolvency proceedings taking place in any other EU Member States. In addition, confirmation is required that the related company's (or group of companies') COMI is situated within the territory of an EU Member State.

Notice Parties

The Companies Act 2014 does not specifically set out who should be notified of a petition being presented to the court to appoint an examiner. However, the court can adjourn the hearing of the petition until any party that is affected by the petition has been given the opportunity to attend the petition hearing. Therefore, no petition will be heard, or examiner appointed, until such time that the affected parties are provided with notice.

Once the petition is heard, the court may direct notice of all future hearings to be served on certain interested parties. These parties would normally include the Revenue Commissioners and may also include (but are not limited to) the company's largest creditor, its invoice-discounting provider, or any fixed-charge holders. The court will set out the timeframe for the notice period, normally 48 hours. This means that the examiner's future reports will be delivered to the notice parties within 48 hours prior to the hearing.

What Happens if the Application Is Unsuccessful?

The court has complete discretion in deciding whether a petition for examinership should be allowed and if the company concerned can enter examinership. Where the court decides not to appoint an examiner, the protection that the company enjoys as soon as the petition is filed in the central office of the court will be automatically lifted from the company. Therefore, creditors can pursue their claims against the company with whatever remedy they consider warranted, i.e. they may seek for a receiver or liquidator to be appointed over the company. While the company can continue to trade once protection is lifted, the reasons for seeking the protection in the first instance will, of course, remain.

There are a number of reasons why a petition may be dismissed by the court:

1. As discussed in Chapter 4, the court will consider, based on the information to hand, whether the company has a reasonable prospect of survival. The court will determine this by considering whether the company can operate as a 'going concern', either in part or as a whole.

2. A receiver may have been appointed over the company for longer than three days (30 days in Cyprus). As discussed in Chapter 2, the legislation is crystal clear that if a receiver stands appointed to the whole or part of the company for at least three days prior to the date of the presentation of the petition for examinership, then the petition will not be considered.

The issue of the receiver being appointed for three days has been considered and determined in court on numerous occasions. Before the 2014 Companies Act, weekends and public holidays were considered to be part of the three days. For example, in the 2012 case of *The Merrow Limited*, involving its wholly owned subsidiary The Belohn Limited, an operator of Foley's licensed premises in central Dublin, Mr Justice Hogan considered the question of when the three-day time period runs from, taking into account Saturday, Sunday and a public holiday. In this particular case, a receiver was appointed on Friday which meant that the expiry date for the presentation of the petition fell the first day of the following week at midnight. Mr Justice Hogan commented:

> "where the time limited by a provision of this Act for the doing of anything expires on a Saturday or Sunday or a public holiday, the time so limited shall extend to and the thing may be done on the first following day that is not a Saturday, a Sunday or a public holiday".

3. The court will not hear a petition for examinership presented by a contingent or prospective creditor (i.e. a creditor whose claim has not yet been determined, e.g. legal case against the company or an insurance matter) until security for costs have been provided to the court and the court finds that it is reasonable.

4. The court will not appoint an examiner where the company concerned has obligations in relation to a bank asset that has been transferred to NAMA, unless the company has submitted a copy of the petition to NAMA and the court has heard from NAMA in making the order.

5. As discussed above, the court may decline to hear, or discontinue, a petition if it appears to the court that the petitioner or independent expert failed to disclose material information or exercise utmost good faith in the preparation and presentation of the petition or independent expert's report. In relation to the examinership of the Zoe Development Limited group of construction-related companies in 2009, collectively referred to as the *Zoe Group*, the petitioner attempted to secure examinership for a second time for the group after the initial petition was dismissed. However, the attempt was deemed unreasonable by the court, Mr Chief Justice Murray commenting as follows when the case was appealed to the Supreme Court:

> "... the petitioner had a full and complete opportunity to present the petition and have it decided on its merits when the first petition was brought. For the reasons explained above, the bringing of a second petition for exactly the same purpose on the basis of material evidence deliberately withheld from the court in the first petition constitutes an abuse of process. In the circumstances of this case I do not think there are any exceptional or excusing circumstances explaining or justifying the bringing of a second petition nor do I consider that there are any other overriding considerations which could lead the court to permit the second petition to proceed."

In dismissing a petition, the court may award costs against the petitioner. Again, this matter is solely at the discretion of the court and will depend on the circumstances surrounding the petition and whether it has been brought with utmost good faith.

An unsuccessful petition does not prevent a company from applying to the court again for protection. However, as can be surmised from the 2009 *Zoe Group* case (see above), reapplication would need to be warranted and supported with concrete reasons to justify a second petition. Although there is nothing in the legislation clearly precluding multiple petitions from being brought, careful consideration would be required before reapplying.

KEY POINTS: THE APPOINTMENT OF AN EXAMINER

1. An examiner is usually an accountant and/or a licensed insolvency practitioner with experience in business restructuring and insolvencies, appointed by the court to a company seeking its protection.
2. The application to appoint an examiner is accompanied by a 'consent to act' presented to the court by the company's nominated examiner together with an affidavit of fitness, usually from a solicitor confirming that the nominated examiner is fit to act as an examiner.
3. A petition seeking court protection must be accompanied by an independent expert's report (IER) prepared by either the auditor of the company or a qualified accountant who is independent of the company.
4. The IER is the main document that the court relies upon in deciding whether to grant court protection. This document's purpose is to demonstrate that the company has a reasonable prospect of survival and that the examinership process will likely be a worthwhile exercise and will yield a greater return to the company's creditors than a winding up of the company.
5. The main sections of the IER are the background to the company, its sources of financial difficulties, taxation liabilities, plans for the company's future, details of the management team, conditions for survival, cash-flow projections for the examinership period, and a statement of affairs on a going-concern and winding-up basis.

6. If a company is filing a petition to the Circuit Court, it must be to the court where the company has its registered office at the time of presenting the petition or where the company has its principal place of business.

7. For international businesses, it is important to consider a company's centre of main interests (COMI) when considering where to undertake insolvency proceedings. This should correspond to where the enterprise conducts the management of its interests on a regular basis.

8. A petition can be presented by either the company, the directors, the members who hold at least 10% of the paid-up shares or the creditors of the company.

9. If the court deems it fit, it may appoint an examiner on an interim basis. The interim examiner must submit a report of the work undertaken during the period of their appointment to the court.

6.

The Role of the Court

- Introduction
- The Court's Role in Granting Protection
- Oversight of the Examinership Process
- Matters on Which the Court Can Provide Direction
- Reviewing the Commercial Judgement of the Examiner
- Considering and Approving Schemes of Arrangements
- Key Point: The Role of the Court

Introduction

The court plays an integral part in an examinership as it oversees the entire process, including the initial decision on whether to grant an Order affording the company court protection. The court's role commences as soon as a petition for examinership has been filed and does not conclude until it has made an Order to approve proposals put forward by an examiner or to remove court protection.

As part of the process to appoint an examiner, the court plays a pre-eminent role. As mentioned in the last chapter, the court hears the petition and decides, based on the application's merits, whether or not a company should enter into examinership and an examiner be appointed. In this chapter, we explore the court's function and examine the interplay between the supervisory role of the court and the work of the examiner.

The Court's Role in Granting Protection

The Ex-Parte Application

The court's first participation in an examination process is to facilitate the hearing of the *ex-parte* application (as discussed in Chapter 5), which is brought by the petitioner seeking to obtain court protection and the appointment of an examiner. During this hearing, counsel for the petitioner sets out the reasons the company is seeking the protection of the court, typically by referring to the independent expert's report (IER) (see Chapter 5), with specific importance being placed on the issues faced by the company that have led to its insolvency and highlighting the reasons the company has a reasonable prospect of survival.

Decision on the Appointment of an Interim Examiner

The court does not have to appoint an examiner to a company at the *ex-parte* application stage. Due to the urgency of the matter, however, the court may appoint an interim examiner. While a company is afforded court protection as soon as petitioning papers have been filed, it is at the court's discretion whether to commence the examiner's work there and then to cover the interim period until the full hearing of the petition is set down.

Direction for Hearing of Petition

At the *ex-parte* application stage of the examination process, if the judge deems the application is in order, the court will set down a date for the full hearing of the application for the appointment of an examiner. It will also give directions in relation to the advertising of the petition in two national newspapers as well as selecting which creditors are to be put on notice of the application.

Notice Party Selection

During the *ex-parte* application, one priority for the court is notice party selection. This involves the selection of certain creditors who must be notified by the company, or its legal representatives, that the petition to appoint an examiner has been filed. Each notice party will receive a full copy of the petition papers, together with details of when the application for the appointment of an examiner is to be heard. The creditors typically chosen include secured creditors, the Revenue Commissioners and key litigation and trade creditors. The purpose of notice party selection is to afford certain creditors the opportunity to attend at court for the application hearing and to have their say on the possible appointment of an examiner.

Hearing of Petition for Examinership

As at the *ex-parte* stage of the process, the hearing of the petition for examinership will involve counsel for the company taking the court through the petition papers, in particular the grounding affidavit and the IER. It is at this stage that the court will decide on whether to confirm the appointment of an examiner or to refuse the application.

Facilitation of Opposing Creditors

If there is a creditor opposing the appointment of an examiner, the court can direct that affidavits be filed by the opposing party and set a future date to return to court where the petitioner and the opposing party will each be heard. It is possible, therefore, that the petition process can be protracted. For example, in the *Cluad Earrai Nual Teoranta* (successful) examinership in 2015, the examiner was only appointed on Day 72 of the 100-day process. Taking into account the urgent nature of the application, in practice the full hearing of the petition usually proceeds expeditiously.

Oversight of the Examinership Process

An important element of the court's role in the examinership process is to provide oversight. In this regard, it will hear from the examiner at various stages and events in the process, examples of which are discussed below.

Extension of Time Applications

Applications by the examiner for extensions of time are normally made on Day 35 and Day 70 of the examinership process. The examiner will deliver an affidavit enclosing a report, including an account of the examiner's work carried out to date and the reasons why an extension of time is required. An example of where a time extension would be required is if the examiner and the leading investor are negotiating terms of an investment agreement (see Chapter 8). Another example is where an investment agreement has been signed but the examiner requires additional time to call a meeting of creditors to present them with the scheme of arrangement (see Chapter 9). The courts are normally willing to grant an extension, particularly when it is evident that an investment in the company is likely.

Hearing Applications for and Awarding Costs

The court plays an integral role in hearing applications for and awarding costs. Applications for costs in an examinership should be heard and decided on when the petition is being heard to appoint the examiner. The court will usually direct that the costs of any application presented to the court be awarded as part of the examinership.

Additionally, in cases where an examinership has been unsuccessful, the court will hear the (former) examiner's application for their costs. This may involve a lengthy hearing if there is a party opposing the application and in these cases various affidavits will be exchanged. The court will set dates on which each party will be heard and when the court's directions on the matter will be decided.

Matters on Which the Court Can Provide Direction

There are a number of matters on which the court can provide direction and some of these are outlined in this section. While this discussion is not exhaustive, it is intended to provide an insight into just some of the matters on which the court can give direction.

Repudiation of Onerous Contracts

As discussed in Chapter 3, a company in examinership can seek the approval of the court to repudiate part or all of an onerous contract in order to facilitate the survival of the company. In this regard, the court can exercise discretion in either allowing or disallowing the repudiation of onerous contracts. It may be the case that the onerous contract is brought to the court's attention in the IER on the presentation of the petition for examinership. For example, from 2007 to 2011 many commercial leases were presented as having terms that were unrealistic in the context of the recession.

In seeking repudiation of a contract (lease), it is important that the applicant puts a quantum on the loss that will be incurred by the creditor (lessor) as a consequence. The court will consider what loss or damage will be incurred by the creditors of a company in examinership, including its landlords or lessors, and either allow or disallow the repudiation of a contract (lease). In *Linen Supply of Ireland Limited* (2010) and *O'Brien's Irish Sandwich Bars Limited* (2009), the court made Orders allowing repudiation of the leases.

Approval of Payment of Pre-Petition Debt

The court has discretion to approve pre-petition debts (i.e. frozen debts incurred by the company before it petitioned the court for protection) that were not recommended for payment in the IER. This issue arises frequently in examinership cases. As discussed in Chapter 5, insurance premiums and employee wages are usually pre-petition payments that are included in the IER and approved by the court at the petitioning stage. However, other *essential* suppliers that require payment may arise during the protection period. The examiner will then be required to make an application to the court and seek its approval in order to discharge the additional pre-petition liabilities.

In the successful 2017 examinership of the *Edward Holdings Group*, 'normal' approval of pre-petition debt was sought by the independent expert in his IER in respect of employee wages and insurance premiums. However, during the course of the examinership, the examiner was required to seek approval for and discharge pre-petition Revenue liabilities in order for certain companies within the group (trading as two hotels and a cinema in Galway city) to renew their liquor licences. The examiner determined, and the court agreed with him, that if the payments were not made to Revenue and the companies' licences were not renewed, this would severely affect the survival prospects of those companies.

Carving Out Fixed Security

The Companies Act 2014 states that the examiner can dispose of or deal with property of the company that is subject to a fixed charge. However, the court must grant authority to the examiner to do so. In considering such an application, the court will consider if the property is dealt with in the way suggested by the examiner the company will still have a prospect of survival as a going concern.

The 'carving out' by the court of fixed security arose during the successful 2013 examinership of *Tougher's Oil Distributors Limited*. In this examinership, the examiner was successful in obtaining an investment package for the trading element of the company. The company had also diversified into property development, which included ownership and management of a business park in Naas, County Kildare. The examiner's scheme of arrangement proposed that one of the company's folios be divided so that the motor fuel forecourt business would be taken over by the investor as part of the trading element of the company to be retained as a going concern; separately, the scheme provided that a receiver be appointed over the remainder of the company's asset portfolio, which included industrial buildings and land. The scheme was formulated in this way with the consent of the fixed-charge holders, one of which was NAMA.

Reviewing the Commercial Judgement of the Examiner

In recent years, the courts have recognised the commercial experience that the examiner can bring to the examinership process and the issues that arise, and have made a number of decisions that reflect the reluctance of the court to interfere with the commercial judgement exercised by the examiner.

The court will only review the commercial judgement of the examiner in a scenario in which it is so "utterly unreasonable and absurd that no reasonable man" would have made the decision that the examiner made. This was the finding of Mr Justice Peter Kelly in the 2012 *Eircom* case, ruling against a challenge to the examiner's selection of the preferred investor in the process. In the *Ladbrokes* case in 2015, the examiner refused to give a potential investor key information which a purported investor claimed they required to enable them to make an informed decision. The examiner and the company claimed that the information was confidential and refusal to provide the information mitigated the risk of such commercially sensitive information being used against the company by unsuccessful bidders in the future. The court determined that the decision by the examiner was within the scope of his commercial judgement.

Considering and Approving Schemes of Arrangements

As we shall see in Chapter 9, the entire examinership is predicated on ultimately securing the approval of the court for the examiner's schemes of arrangement. Some of the steps taken by the court include the following:
- accepting the final report of the examiner;
- setting a date for the hearing to approve the scheme of arrangement;
- approving the scheme and setting its effective date;
- delivering judgment.

A meeting of creditors will be held and if the scheme of arrangement is approved by at least one class of creditor, the examiner will lodge his or her report with the court immediately. The court will then set down a date for the consideration of the proposals put forward in the scheme of arrangement.

Before the court confirms or accepts the proposals, it must be satisfied that the following criteria have been met:
- at least one class of creditors whose interests or claims would be impaired by the implementation of the proposals must have voted to accept the proposals (in practice, the court will look at what the popular view of creditors is across the classes);
- the proposals must be fair and equitable in relation to any class of members or creditors that have not accepted the proposals and whose interests or claims would be impaired by their implementation;
- the proposals do not have as their primary purpose the avoidance of taxes;
- the proposals must not be unfairly prejudicial to the interests of any interested party.

However, these factors (sometimes referred to as the 'gating' mechanism) only serve to trigger the ability of the presiding judge to exercise their discretion regarding the approval of the scheme of arrangement. The court has the power to confirm, confirm subject to modification, or refuse the proposals. Although the court has very wide ranging powers to make modifications to proposals, in practice it will not rewrite a scheme of arrangement.

If the scheme is approved, the court will set down a date when the scheme of arrangement comes into effect. This is known as the 'effective date' of the scheme. Securing an effective date for their court-approved scheme of arrangement is the aim of every examiner from the moment they are appointed.

Key Points: The Role of the Court

1. The court's first function in an examinership is to facilitate the hearing of the petition seeking to obtain court protection and the appointment of an examiner.
2. The court gives the petitioner directions in relation to the advertising of the petition in two national newspapers as well as selecting which creditors are to be put on notice of the application.
3. If a creditor opposes the appointment of an examiner, affidavits can be filed by the opposing party and the court will set a future date to return to court for a hearing.
4. The court will review the examiner's reports made on Day 35 and Day 70, in order to decide whether to extend the examinership process. Granting an extension is dependent on how likely it is that there will be a scheme of arrangement for the company in examinership.
5. If the examiner recommends the repudiation of all or part of an onerous contract, the court will consider the loss incurred by the creditors and either allow or disallow the repudiation.
6. The court has the discretion to approve pre-petition debts relating to suppliers that are essential for the company's survival.
7. The court will ensure that the examiner's scheme of arrangement is fair, equitable and not unfairly prejudicial to any party involved in the process before considering its approval.

7.

The Role of the Examiner

- Introduction
- Review and Validation
- Communication throughout the Examinership
- Responsibility of the Company/Management in Examinership
- Reporting to the Court and Seeking Extensions
- Reporting to the Office of the Director of Corporate Enforcement (ODCE)
- Monitoring Key Aspects of the Business
- Investigations by the Examiner
- Executive Powers
- Continuing to Trade
- "In examination under Part 10 of the Companies Act 2014"
- Key Points: The Role of the Examiner

Introduction

Aspects of the role of the examiner have already been discussed in various chapters of this book. While the role of the examiner can vary widely between cases, there are certain critical duties an examiner must always fulfill. The various facets of acting as an examiner are set out in this chapter. They are also reflected in the 'Examinership Timeline' provided in Appendix C.

Review and Validation

The Early Days of the Examinership

It is rare that an examiner will be appointed to a company without having met the directors at least once. It is normal for an examiner to engage with directors for a period before appointment so that the examiner can assess whether it is appropriate for him or her to consent to act.

Immediately after an examiner is appointed, they will typically look to meet with the directors of the company with a view to carrying out an initial high-level review of the issues likely to be critical for the examinership. The business will inevitably be in crisis at this time and there will certainly be an array of very pressing matters for the examiner, including meeting with key staff (or perhaps all staff) and key customers and suppliers/creditors. Week 1, particularly Day 1, of an examinership is typically the busiest period as the examiner deals with pressing issues and gets to know the business and all its moving parts.

An examiner, together with their staff, will attend the company's main business premises on Day 1 to familiarise themselves with the company and its operations and, more importantly, to explain the process to the employees and answer any queries they may have, such as about the future of the company, payment of wages, etc. Members of the examiner's staff will take note of stock, assets and other financial information.

From the outset, it is important for the examiner to quickly establish a good working relationship with the company's board of directors. The examiner does not normally usurp the decision-making of the board, though they can preside over board meetings with an agenda that they have set. Typically, therefore, the examiner exerts a huge influence over the company during the restructuring process. It is a role that, in practical terms regarding the trade of the business, is akin to the role of a strong non-executive chair.

When the petition of examinership is presented, the company's directors will normally be under huge personal pressure and their thinking may be clouded or even irrational. The examiner's challenge in these early days is to ensure that the directors are focused on stabilising the company's operations and ensuring that, as far as possible, it is 'business as usual' for staff and customers. Critically, the examiner must instil a positive sense that the company has now entered a short restructuring and reorganisation phase that will result in a scheme of arrangement with its creditors and the survival of the business. An examiner will often enter a company where hope is in short supply and the examiner and the examiner's team must work hard to ensure that the people involved in the business focus on its survival.

Reviewing Assertions in the Petition and Independent Expert's Report

The examiner will have been appointed by the court on the basis of various assertions made in the petition for examinership and in the independent expert's report (IER). In the early days of the examinership, the examiner will check the factual basis of these assertions, upon which the fate of the company is likely to depend. For example, there will have been statements regarding the company's continuing ability to trade, whether it can source materials, resources and services from suppliers and the likely cashflow available from sales in the early weeks of the examinership. In short, the examiner will carry out a 'reality check' to ensure that the company does have a reasonable prospect of survival, the key test required by the legislation, as discussed in Chapter 4.

While the independent expert in their IER will have 'looked back' to establish the causes of the company's insolvency and whether its assets are satisfactorily accounted for, the examiner tends to look forward to the likely formulation of a scheme of arrangement and a proposal for investment. The examiner must also be vigilant and monitor the company's position carefully in the early days of the examinership as under the legislation they are obliged to return to court immediately if the company is in fact doomed to fail and there is no longer any basis for the continued court protection. Best practice is for the examiner to take the 10-week cash-flow projection as set out in the IER (discussed in Chapter 5) and compare these on a week-by-week basis with the actual cashflows.

Removal of Court Protection

Variances between the cash-flow projections set out in the IER and actual weekly results warrant careful investigation by the examiner. The first court report required from the examiner within 35 days (or at the full hearing of the petition if an interim examiner has been appointed, as discussed in Chapter 6) will typically explain any negative variances and reassure the court that the company is still capable of survival.

If the company is not capable of survival, then the examiner must apprise the court of this fact and ask for court protection to be removed. In this scenario:

* the company will typically move into a receivership phase (if a secured creditor decides to appoint a receiver); or
* the court will appoint an official liquidator; or
* the directors will immediately call a creditors' meeting to wind up the company.

On rare occasions, an alternative outcome to those listed above will arise with the removal of court protection. In the 2011 examinership of *Whitfield Clinic*, a private hospital in Waterford, where court protection was granted to the parent company Euro Care International Ltd and a number of its subsidiaries, Euro Care Healthcare Ltd, Euro Care Property Management Ltd and Euro Care Infrastructure Ltd, the examinership only lasted a short number of days before the examiner returned to court to have protection removed on patient safety grounds based on the recommendation of the clinicians at the hospital. In this instance, the secured creditor did not appoint a receiver, but rather, a receiver was appointed over the shares of the borrower, an extraordinary general meeting (EGM) was called and a new board of directors installed.

Another, more recent example of court protection being withdrawn occurred in 2018 during the examinership of the Dublin toy distributor *Yvolve Sports Limited*, when an entrenched shareholder dispute was finally settled in the opening weeks of the process. The withdrawal of court protection was followed by the recapitalisation of the company outside examinership with, unusually, all creditors being paid in full and, critically, all of the jobs of the 50 employees being maintained.

Communication throughout the Examinership

Communication is an important part of the examiner's role as it allows the examiner to identify any issues that need to be addressed to allow the company to trade successfully into the future.

The Appointment of the Examiner

In Ireland, a Form E24 (Notice of petition for appointment of examiner) must be delivered to the Companies Registration Office (CRO) within three days of the petition's presentation to the court. Once appointed, the examiner is obliged to ensure that all notification obligations as set out in the legislation and as required by the court are adhered to. In Ireland, the examiner must:

- deliver a copy of the Order for their appointment to the CRO within three days of that appointment;
- publish a notice of their appointment in *Iris Oifigiúil* (the official Irish state gazette) within 21 days of that appointment;
- publish notice of their appointment in two national daily newspapers within 21 days. This must be circulated in the district in which the company's registered office is located or where the company carries out its principal activity.

In Cyprus, the examiner must:

- within three days of their appointment deliver a copy of the petition to the Register of Companies, as well as any other notice party as directed by the court;
- within 21 days of their appointment publish a copy of the appointment notice in the Cyprus Government Gazette;
- deliver a copy of the order appointing them as examiner to the Land Registry Office within three days of their appointment.

Methods of Communication

Throughout the period of examinership, the examiner will communicate with creditors, directors and shareholders through written correspondence, meetings and on-site visits.

Written Correspondence   Once an examiner is appointed over a company, they will list all parties potentially affected by the examinership and will write to each of them. Such parties will include:

- secured and unsecured creditors, including, but not limited to, leasing creditors;
- shareholders;
- directors;
- the Revenue Commissioners (Revenue);
- invoice discounting providers;
- the company's bank(s);
- providers of utilities such as electricity, water and telephones;
- insurance providers; and
- any other party deemed affected.

Such correspondence will set out:

- the date of the examiner's appointment;
- a short briefing about the examinership process;

106

- the contact details of someone in the examiner's office to whom any queries can be directed; and
- a request to submit any outstanding claims against the company before the date that court protection was granted.

The correspondence with all the parties affected by the process concludes with the examiner's proposals, setting out the treatment of the various classes of creditors in the proposed scheme of arrangement (see Chapter 9).

Throughout the examinership process, the examiner will receive and respond to correspondence, which may be with the legal advisors of creditors submitting their claims against the company in examinership.

Meetings   On Day 1, the examiner and their team will attend the company's premises to meet with the directors, management and staff. The examiner will explain the examinership process to all concerned and answer questions.

In order to gain more of an understanding of the company and business, the examiner will also meet with:
- the finance department to establish the software being used to record and manage the finances;
- the payroll person to establish the timing of payments to employees and the system used to record same;
- the production manager to establish the process of production, to try to establish future needs, projections and requirements;
- the sales team to establish how sales are secured, and to estimate future projections;
- the directors and shareholders to establish whether there are any communication barriers between them, or if there are any shareholder disputes that might prevent the examiner from performing his or her duties;
- the company's landlord, if applicable, to discuss and identify any issues that may arise during examinership;
- the company's invoice-discounting provider to agree terms for the period of the examinership.

Site Visits   It is important that an examiner and their team attend the company on a regular basis to meet with staff members, the finance team, and any suppliers or customers that wish to meet them. During an examinership, the examiner and their staff may attend on site more frequently than usual at a request of an interested party. This happened in the 2018 examinership of *Ryco Book Protection Services*, a manufacturer of products for the protection of hardback and paperback books based in County Wicklow, where the company's invoice discounter insisted a member of the examiner's team attend on site, review the invoices that were being financed and ensure that correct procedures for debtor collection were in place.

There may be other reasons why more regular site visits are important. In the 2018 case, *Basta Parsons Limited*, the company in examinership needed to be environmentally audited from time to time due to contamination issues at the company premises. The examiner met and worked with a representative from the Environmental Protection Agency (EPA) to establish the current environmental issues and, in particular, to adjudicate on the contingent liabilities of the site. The examiner then included these costs as part of his proposals for a scheme of arrangement.

Responsibility of the Company/Management in Examinership

The appointment of an examiner should not affect the day-to-day management or running of the company. The examiner is an officer of the court and not the company; therefore, the management and control of the company still vests with its directors. As mentioned previously in this chapter, however, the examiner does have certain powers when it comes to presiding over board meetings.

The company, including its management, should assist the examiner in examining the affairs of the company. Below is a non-exhaustive list of the assistance that can be provided by the company in this regard:

- access to the company's premises;
- supply of financial documents when required;
- assist with due diligence documentation that may be required from a potential investor;
- communicating to the examiner any concerns regarding trading, cash flow, stock, etc.;
- attending meetings with the examiner;
- continuing with normal, day-to-day activities in order to ensure that the company successfully exits examinership.

Reporting to the Court and Seeking Extensions

As outlined in Chapter 9, where an application for the appointment of an examiner is successful, an examiner must, as soon as practically possible after their appointment, formulate proposals for a compromise with creditors called 'a scheme of arrangement' in relation to the company concerned. The duty of the examiner is to conduct an examination of the affairs of the company and report to the court within 35 days of their appointment (or such longer period as the court may allow – see below).

Thus, the examiner will be given an initial period of 35 days from the date of their appointment to return to court with an update on the examinership. Initially, the examiner may present a report to the court before or within 35 days of their appointment setting out a scheme of arrangement as being confirmed. However, in most cases, the examiner will attend court within that period to seek an extension within which to prepare the scheme. The documents and information required for this extension include:

1. an affidavit of the examiner requesting an extension of time;
2. a report exhibited to the affidavit detailing the following:
   ○ an introductory paragraph setting the chronology of events regarding the timeframe for which the examiner was originally appointed (as the judge hearing the matter may not be familiar with the case);
   ○ background information on the company;
   ○ a summary of the conditions for survival of the company as per the IER;
   ○ a summary of work carried out from the appointment date to the date of the report, including work relating to:
     ◆ Day 1 tasks carried out;
     ◆ banking arrangements and any issues with same;
     ◆ how the company's trade has performed in the opening weeks of the examinership;
     ◆ how the investment process for the company is progressing, or whether it is likely the scheme of arrangement will be funded in some other way;
     ◆ an update on the creditor position, especially if there are creditors that have come to light who were not included in the IER;
     ◆ the results of any stocktake carried out, with specific reference to creditors that have claims for retention of title over that stock;
     ◆ any correspondence with the Revenue Commissioners;
     ◆ any other issues that are significant.

If the extension of the protection period is granted, the examinership will continue generally up to Day 70 of the examinership by which time it is expected that the examiner will formulate their scheme or arrangement. Nearing the end of the extended period, if a scheme is nearly finalised but more time is required to arrange the creditors' meetings (with three days' notice), concluding certain issues and other technicalities, the examiner would tend to apply for a further extension up to Day 100. In this case, the report accompanying the examiner's affidavit will set out similar information as their initial report but will focus more on the reasons for the extension, particularly how the investment process is progressing, for example required negotiations with a preferred investor to iron out final issues and any additional funding to be generated from:

- disposal of non-core assets;
- leverage of valuable non-secured assets;
- collections of protracted insurance claims; or
- collection of Revenue refunds.

If an application is made for further time beyond Day 70, the examiner must be satisfied that the extension will facilitate the formulation of proposals and the matters delaying the formulation of proposals must be outlined to the court.

In recent years, particular focus has been placed on the ability of an examiner to efficiently advance matters so that examinerships can be concluded at an earlier stage rather than towards the end of the 100-day period. This aligns with the purpose of the legislation such that an extension beyond Day 70 should be granted only in circumstances where the examiner is satisfied that it will be possible to formulate proposals if further time is granted.

Utmost Good Faith of the Examiner

A vital duty of an examiner is to always act with utmost good faith in reports to the court. The integrity of the examinership process depends on full and frank disclosure of all material facts to the court. Numerous cases have reinforced the crucial importance of the examiner acting with full candour, including *Wogans (Drogheda) Limited* (1992) and *Camden Street Taverns Limited* (2013).

Reporting to the ODCE

Since the implementation of the Companies Act 2014, the Office of the Director of Corporate Enforcement (ODCE) has taken a more active role in the examinership process. It is now necessary to keep the ODCE informed about developments in the examinership. The ODCE writes to the examiner requesting the reasons that the company has entered examinership and information about the role of the directors in that process. The ODCE will also request the following documentation and the examiner is expected to respond in a timely manner:

- a copy of the petition documents, including the IER;
- a copy of the last full set of financial statements prepared for the company;
- a copy of the last set of management accounts prepared by the company;

- a copy of the examiner's report to the court (see above) and any other information requested by the court;
- any other information the ODCE deems necessary.

Monitoring Key Aspects of the Business

An examiner must act independently of the company, its board of directors, shareholders, creditors or prospective investors. Although the directors retain their positions, the examiner holds a position whereby they oversee and monitor certain aspects of the business, exercising professional judgement for the best possible outcome for the stakeholders. The key elements of the business typically monitored by the examiner are discussed below.

Cash Flow

As discussed in Chapter 3, a company seeks the protection of the court in an examinership in order to provide breathing space from the debts it has generated and, in turn, the creditors who are demanding payment. The examinership period of protection allows the business to concentrate on regularising its cash flow and to realistically assess:
1. viable income, i.e. what is realistic in terms of sales over the period of protection; and
2. outgoings that are essential, plus any that may no longer be required (this would cover any creditors prior to the date of petition).

The court protection allows the company space and time to come to new arrangements with existing suppliers or possibly source alternative suppliers.

The examiner's role includes monitoring cash flow on a weekly basis, working from the cash-flow projections in the IER and comparing these with actual, weekly cash flow. Trends in income, expenditure, incomings and debtors will also be considered.

As cash flow forms part of the examiner's reports to the court on the examinership's progress, explanations will be sought from management about any variances and action will be taken where necessary. As discussed in Chapter 4, for an enterprise to be a suitable candidate for examinership, it is necessary to demonstrate to the court that it can trade broadly in line with the projections set out in the IER; this will assist the company in validating one of the key indicators that it has a strong prospect of survival.

Stocktakes/Retention of Title Claims

Depending on the type of business and industry involved, stock may be a key asset of the company. Therefore, an accurate stocktake will be required. On Day 1 of an examinership, the examiner will request the current management of the company to carry out a stocktake of the company's stock and assets in order to establish their levels.

A full stocktake will also help the examiner deal with any claims for retention of title (ROT) from creditors during the period of examinership. The examiner will establish the level of ROT claims by creditors and these will be a separate class of creditor in the scheme of arrangement. As a company is under the protection of the court, technically a ROT creditor is not entitled to recover their stock or leased assets. However, this is at the discretion of the examiner, who, depending on the circumstances, may release the stock or assets.

Debtors (including Invoice-discounting Providers)

It is important that, during the examinership period, debtors are collected in the normal manner and under the normal terms. This is to ensure that projections for the examinership period, as referred to in the IER, are turned into actuals, which will strengthen the company's cash-flow position. Collecting debts and indeed negotiating early payment can be of great benefit to the cash flow. It is important for the examiner to be satisfied regarding the accuracy of the company's debtor ledger. There are numerous examples of examinership cases in recent years where the directors, under significant personal pressure, have invoiced certain customers in advance, or indeed invoiced customers that do not exist at all, with the intent of raising finance on those invoices in a desperate attempt to keep the company alive. If there are any matters for concern or unusual trends, the examiner may convene a meeting of the board of directors and relevant management. This will certainly be highlighted in the examiner's report to the court.

Where a company is relying on certain facilities, e.g. invoice discounting, it is important to commence communication with the provider as soon as the appointment is made by the court. This is in order to establish terms applicable during the examination period and to explore other options of generating cash from other facilities offered by the invoice-discounting provider, e.g. asset-based lending or a trade facility. Depending on the level of cash being injected into a company during the protection period, the invoice-discounting provider may insist that the examiner verify the accuracy of the invoices being generated by the company.

This issue was explored in the 2018 case of *Yvolve Sports Limited*, where the company relied heavily on its invoice-discounting provider. The examiner, the company and the invoice discounter discussed various options to provide the company with cash flow to ensure the company could meet the IER trading projections. During the examinership, a novel way of raising finance was identified in the form of a supplier payment trade facility, which released funds on the basis of purchase order numbers and shipping documents for goods coming from China.

Tax Compliance

Revenue Involvement   Regardless of the level of the debt involved, Revenue will be actively involved as a creditor in the examinership process and therefore will be one of the expected notice parties.

It is essential for a company in examinership to ensure that it is compliant in filing tax returns and discharging taxes as they fall due. Failure to comply may cause Revenue to object to any of the following:
* the appointment of an examiner to the company;
* the extension of the protection period (see "Reporting to the Court and Seeking Extensions" above);
* proposals for and confirmation of a scheme of arrangement between the company and its creditors and/or members.

Revenue Returns and Liabilities   The debt owing to Revenue, like all other creditor balances, is separated into the following categories:
* pre-petition liabilities – any unpaid super preferential employee PRSI, preferential taxes and unsecured tax liabilities incurred prior to the petition for examinership being presented;
* post-petition liabilities – any liabilities incurred during the period of protection, which will be payable as normal.

If there are any returns to Revenue outstanding after the petition has been approved, Revenue will request that these are brought up to the petition date as soon as the examiner is appointed. The examiner will work with the company's in-house finance department or its accountant, if the function is outsourced, and/or directors to ensure that such returns are filed and will obtain copies of the filed returns. It is important to remember that no pre-petition tax liabilities will be paid when filing the pre-petition returns. These pre-petition tax liabilities will form part of the scheme of arrangement that will be proposed at a meeting of creditors, if such a scheme can be put together.

The court will generally direct, by an Order, that all post-petition tax returns and liabilities are filed and paid as they fall due. Therefore, it is essential for the company to take account of this in the cash-flow projections provided in the IER and ensure they are paid as they fall due. All post-petition returns need to be filed and paid on time to Revenue.

Tax Clearance Certificates   A tax clearance certificate is an essential document to be eligible to provide goods and services to public sector bodies. It is important to note that Revenue may rescind a company's tax clearance certificate once it is under the protection of the court in examinership. However, the examiner can apply for a temporary tax clearance certificate. Revenue will deal with such applications on a case-by-case basis and the period that the tax clearance covers will be at the discretion of Revenue. In the case of *Regan Development Limited* in 2017, Revenue issued the company a tax clearance certificate on a month-to-month basis, ensuring that the company's post-petition tax returns and liabilities were up to date.

Liabilities During the Period of Examinership

Similar to the distinction between a company's pre- and post-petition tax liabilities, its debts to its creditors are distinguished as pre- and post-petition liabilities.

Pre-Petition Liabilities   Any liabilities arising from the provision of either goods or services to the company prior to the date of its successful petition for examinership will form part of a proposed scheme of arrangement with its creditors, which will be put together by the examiner, subject to sufficient funding being available.

As discussed in Chapter 5, though the payment of pre-petition liabilities is prevented by the appointment of an examiner, where the IER includes a recommendation to discharge or satisfy, in whole or in part, a liability deemed essential for the continuity of the business, such as employees' wages, insurance or utility charges, such a liability should be discharged. There are a number of types of suppliers that may fall under this exception and this should be considered on a case-by-case basis.

When the examiner believes that it is essential and warranted that a particular supplier be paid in preference to others, he or she will have to make an application to the court seeking authorisation to discharge such liability, stating any compelling reasons. If the court is satisfied that a failure to discharge or satisfy, in whole or in part, that liability would considerably reduce the prospects of the company (or the whole or any parts of its undertakings) surviving as a going concern, the court has the jurisdiction to authorise such applications. There is also a provision in the Companies Act allowing for any interested party to be heard or indeed object to such an application to the court.

In the 2018 examinership of *Denis Moriarty The Kerries Limited*, a civil contractor specialising in the construction of wind farms, the examiner sought approval from the court to discharge a number of liabilities owing to suppliers of materials and to the company's architect. The examiner determined that these payments were essential to the survival prospects of the company as without them the suppliers would not have released materials necessary to conclude a contract and the architect would not have certified the company's work, resulting in the company not being paid for that work. The court agreed with the examiner's conclusion and approved payment of the pre-petition liabilities. The company successfully exited the examinership process in May 2018.

Post-petition Liabilities These liabilities arise from either goods or services supplied to the company after the presentation of the petition for examinership to the court. Such payments can be made during the protection period and typically under the company's normal terms of business, though some suppliers to companies under examinership change their payment terms during the protection period in order to minimise their exposure. A company in examinership and its creditors must find a balance in relation to business terms and creditor terms in order to ensure continuity of trade during the period of examinership.

As discussed in Chapter 5, during the examinership, the examiner will monitor and question any variances between the business's forecasted and actual cash flows. In doing so, the examiner can review the level of debt incurred by the company during the protection period and encourage sustainable debt models, for example avoiding extensive credit terms with suppliers and excessive inventory. This will help a company exiting examinership to continue to trade on a sustainable basis.

Investigations by the Examiner

Under company law, directors primarily have fiduciary and statutory duties to the company and its shareholders, and they are required to understand and act on these duties. However, this principle evolves when a company becomes insolvent. The duty to act in good faith and to show the utmost care, skill and diligence will instead be primarily owed by the directors to the company's creditors rather than its shareholders. This is not always understood by directors, leading to issues that must be investigated by the examiner, some of the key ones of which are discussed below. The examiner must immediately report back to the court where they believe that the directors are not acting in the utmost good faith.

Fraudulent Trading

If any person is knowingly a party to the carrying on of the business of a company with the intent to defraud its creditors, or the creditors of any other person, or any other fraudulent purpose, they may be guilty of fraudulent trading. This offence can manifest itself in a number of ways, including, but not limited to:

- diverting monies payable to the company to a director or shareholder;
- incurring credit at a time when to the knowledge of the director there is no prospect of that credit being repayable;
- non-payment of monies to employees or to pension funds.

A person, while acting as an officer a company engaged in fraudulent activities, may be personally responsible for all or any of the debts of the company as the court may direct in accordance with section 610 of the Companies Act 2014.

Asset Movements

An examiner can apply to the court for the return of property disposed of by the company if they consider that the intent of the disposal was to disadvantage the company, its creditors or members. Where the court is satisfied of this, it may order the return of the property or the proceeds from its sale.

An example of this was in the 2009 examinership of *Chartbusters Limited* and its related companies, where a DVD rental and retail store in Swords, County Dublin, had been transferred to a company outside the group. The examiner succeeded in getting the Swords store, the group's most profitable, transferred back to the group as it was essential for the company's survival.

In the 2010 examinership of *Mediterranean Food & Wine Limited* ('MFWL'), a company operating the Zumo chain of juice and smoothie bars, certain creditors of the company made a claim indicating that they were prejudiced by the restructuring of the business, which took place between 2007 and 2009. The restructuring included the transfer from MFWL of intellectual property relating to the Zumo franchise business to a related company. The examiner investigated this matter and, after reviewing the restructuring, was satisfied that no prejudice existed to the creditors of the business from the restructuring as a result of the level of secured debt and the consent given at the time by the charge-holder, i.e. the chargeholder was in agreement with the restructuring at the time it took place. The conclusion of this investigation was reported back to the presiding judge (Mr Justice Frank Clarke, now Chief Justice), who was satisfied with the examiner's findings.

Reckless Trading

If, in the course of an examinership, or where an insolvent company is being wound up, it is found that any director or officer of the company was knowingly a party to the carrying on of the business in a reckless manner, then such person may be personally liable for all or any part of the debts or other liabilities of the company. In practice, it can be difficult to prove this within 100 days.

A director or officer of a company is knowingly a party to the carrying on of any business of the company in a reckless manner where, given that they have the knowledge, skills and experience of running a business that might reasonably be expected of a person in that position, they ought to have known that their actions or those of the company would cause loss to any creditor, or where they were a party to the contracting of new company debt and did not honestly believe on reasonable grounds that the company would be able to discharge those debts when falling due.

For a director or officer of the company to be held culpable of reckless trading, they must have had knowledge that their actions would cause loss to creditors. There is a very fine line between this and fraudulent behaviour. It is not a legitimate defence on the part of a director or other officer that they were uncertain about the company's finances. In addition, they cannot state that they acted honestly and responsibly if they did not keep themselves informed of the company's affairs. Therefore, failure to actively take part in the affairs of the company may not provide relief from personal liability, as the failure to exercise proper control may amount to recklessness.

Directors' Conduct

Regrettably, a relatively common feature of examinership cases in recent years has been poor performance by company directors, and in many instances disharmony at board level has led to crisis within the business. The examiner can also report to the court about the conduct of directors and make recommendations regarding the future management of the business in the ultimate scheme of arrangement. As we have seen in this chapter, an examiner has the power to convene, set the agenda for, and preside at meetings of the board of directors and general meetings of the company to which they are appointed, and to propose motions or resolutions and to report to such meetings. The examiner is also entitled to receive reasonable notice of, to attend and be heard at, all meetings of the board and all general meetings of the company. If the examiner concludes during the examinership that the directors' conduct is a concern, then executive powers can be applied for and the court can grant these. This allows the examiner to have the same powers as the directors and run the company.

In the 2016 examinership of *Business Mobile Security Services Limited*, a multi-disciplinary security services and cash-in-transit business, having applied successfully to the court, the examiner took over certain executive functions of the company as a result of shareholder and management disputes. One of the main reasons for the failure of the company and for its seeking court protection was a complete breakdown in trust and communication between two sets of the directors and shareholders. The company's directors also consented to the application, having signed a board resolution the previous day acknowledging that proper controls were not in place and that in order to safeguard the client funds, the examiner should take over these executive functions.

In addition, if the examiner becomes aware of any variation in the company's assets, income or liabilities that is vital to the company's prospect of survival then there exists the power to take whatever steps are necessary in good faith to halt, prevent or rectify the detrimental effects of same. The examiner may also apply to the court to determine any question arising in the course of the appointment.

The examiner also has the power to compel all directors of the company to provide all of the assistance that they are reasonably able to give, including providing the examiner with the books and records of the company and answering queries the examiner may have in relation to same.

Executive Powers

As discussed above, during the period that the company is under the protection of the court, the directors retain all their executive powers. However, there are provisions in the legislation allowing the examiner, under certain circumstances, to apply to the court to have all or some of the functions vested in the directors performable only by the examiner. The court will not revoke and transfer all or some directors' executive powers without reasonable cause and will carefully consider how such a decision would affect the day-to-day running of the company. Each case will be heard on its merits and the court may grant such an order in order to:

- prevent the interests of the company, its employees or its creditors as a whole being prejudiced by the way the affairs of the company are being conducted or are likely to be conducted;
- preserve the assets of the company;
- safeguard the interests of the company, its employees or creditors by curtailing or regulating the company's directors or management in carrying out the business of the company or the performance of their functions.

The court may extend the powers of the examiner to those equivalent of a liquidator's, as if they were a liquidator of the company appointed by the court. These powers include, but are not limited to, the power to dispose of company assets, repudiate contracts and ensure the return of improperly transferred assets. If the court directs that the examiner should be given such powers, the examiner must report to the court if matters come to light throughout the process that warrant court direction; for example, the examiner might report to the court seeking direction on an investigation that they have concluded as part of the process.

In the 2017 case of *Quesada Developments*, when the petition for examinership was heard, the court directed that the examiner appointed would have the power to file the company's financial statements and annual return with the CRO, convene and preside over board meetings, and direct day-to-day finance matters, including the weekly payroll. The examiner was in a position to obtain a tax clearance certificate from Revenue and request payments from the Health Services Executive.

There are a number of reasons an examiner may seek to have and perform executive functions in a company. The case of *Business Mobile Security Services Limited* discussed above has already highlighted some of these in respect of the finance function. In the 2017 examinership of *Edward Holdings Group* and related companies, the examiner sought executive powers in respect of executing the investment documentation, namely the investment and escrow agreements (see Chapter 8). Executive powers were sought in this instance because the preferred investor was an external, unconnected party to the existing shareholders and directors of the companies, and the examiner had not received the necessary assurances that the directors would execute the investment documentation. The executive powers were obtained from the court and the companies successfully emerged from the examination process.

Continuing to Trade

In order for a company to successfully trade out of examinership, it must continue to trade during the examinership and existing supplier relationships usually must be maintained. In this section, we discuss aspects of a business that are central to its continuity of trade and when exiting the examinership process.

Staff

As outlined in Chapter 1, a key reason a company will choose the examinership option over liquidation is to save jobs and retain staff. By entering examinership, the company is, with the help of the examiner, committing to continuing the business successfully into the future.

We saw at the start of this chapter how the examiner will meet with staff on Day 1 of the examinership to explain the process and answer any questions. Typically, day-to-day roles and jobs will not change, nor will the reporting structure. However, if the examiner is granted any executive power or function (see above), the reporting structure of the business will change. In the *Quesada Developments* case, the examiner was given executive functions, which entailed that the examiner's office assisted with payroll, finance discussions and staffing requirements. (It is important to note that although the examiner is involved in such decision making, they will often look to the company's management for assistance and advice.)

Lenders and Banks

A bank or finance institution is not obliged to work with a company in examinership. It is particularly important to note that if a company's current account is overdrawn and another account belonging to the company is in credit, the bank has authority to offset the positive balance with the negative balance. This may have serious repercussions for the company in examinership and affect the working capital of the company. Therefore, it will need to be considered by the company prior to presenting a petition for examinership to the court.

A very welcome practical development in recent years has been the willingness of banks and other financial institutions to advance fresh funding to help facilitate a scheme of arrangement for a company in examinership. The 2020 examinership of *Dublin Food Sales Limited* is an example of where a company funded its exit from examinership using both fresh equity and new borrowings from its existing pillar bank. A lack of availability of rescue finance was one of the early predicted weaknesses of the examinership process when it was introduced in 1990. However, if the company is fundamentally sound and has security available, recent evidence suggests that it should be in a position to raise new funding that can lead to a second chance for the business.

Taxation

As mentioned previously, the examiner will continuously liaise with Revenue, which will usually be a notice party in the process. The court will normally make an order that all tax returns are brought up to the date of commencement of the examinership, all returns going forward are filed on time and all liabilities occurring during the period of protection are discharged.

Examiner's Certification of Liabilities

One of the key factors in a company trading successfully through examinership is the ability to continue to source raw materials and supplies. It can be of great assistance to the company that there are circumstances during the protection period where the examiner will certify certain liabilities that are deemed vital for the survival of the company as a going concern. These expenses/liabilities then form part of the examiner's expenses which would have priority payment in a scheme of arrangement, thereby giving additional comfort to the supplier about continuing to supply an insolvent company. Certified liabilities rank ahead of all creditors (with the exception of fixed-charge creditors) in the event the examinership fails and the company goes into receivership or liquidation.

Though examiner's certification does provide comfort to creditors to continue to trade with the company throughout the period of protection, the examiner should also carefully and cautiously consider certifying liabilities as the court has jurisdiction to disallow the payment of certified liabilities.

The examiner will consider the liabilities of the company during the protection period and decide what should be certified. The key issue is to consider whether the company's survival as a going concern during the protection period would be prejudiced if the liabilities were not certified. In the examinership of *Edenpark Construction Limited* in 1994, Mr Justice Murphy stated:

> "It follows, therefore, that to elevate liabilities of the company to the status of expenses of the examiner the following must occur: 1. The liabilities must be certified by the examiner to have

been incurred in circumstances where the survival of the company as a going concern would otherwise be seriously prejudiced; 2. The prejudice must be foreseen as occurring in the period which commenced with the appointment of the examiner and terminating with the cessation of the protection; 3. The certification by the examiner must take place at the time when the liabilities are incurred. Thus, it can be said at once that a liability incurred by a company in procuring the appointment of an examiner could not be a 'certifiable' liability as the relevant period would not have commenced when the liability was incurred."

Liabilities that are required to be certified by the examiner must be done so in the following manner:
• by letter, in writing;
• during the protection period;
• at the time they were incurred;
• on the basis of the examiner's opinion that not certifying such liabilities would seriously prejudice the survival of the company during the protection period;
• identifying the particular goods and services to be supplied and certified;
• indicating that the certificate is given pursuant to the specific section of the Companies Act that deals with certification (currently section 529 of the Companies Act 2014, this was originally section 10 of the Companies (Amendment) Act 1990).

In practical terms, a certificate is a letter to the supplier from the examiner, headed clearly with the relevant section of the Companies Act, confirming that the goods or services just received are certified. Not only can goods or services be certified; actual funds introduced can also be subject to certification. The examiner should retain all documentation surrounding a certification, including invoices and contracts. The question of what liabilities can be certified by an examiner has been contentious over the past number of years and it is evident that such a decision is not straightforward or to be taken lightly.

There are many examples of liabilities being certified by an examiner. In the *Yvolve Sports Limited* case, certification of liabilities was issued by the examiner to both the shareholders for funds introduced and the invoice-discounting provider. These certificates were essential for the release of stock from factories in order to maintain existing contacts and for the business to continue to trade.

In another case in 2017, letters certifying certain of Galvanic Limited's liabilities were issued by the examiner to a director and shareholder as they had personally paid wages for the period of the examinership as recommended by the IER.

Pre-Petition Liabilities of Trade Creditors

As discussed briefly above, pre-petition liabilities should not be discharged by the company as they will be covered by the scheme of arrangement (see Chapter 9). However, the IER may have made a recommendation to discharge a pre-petition liability as doing so is deemed vital for the survival of the company. This is often the case for employees' wages, insurance premiums or utility bills.

In relation to hire-purchase agreements, or goods supplied under similar arrangements, suppliers will not have recourse to normal remedies when attempting to recover their debt. These types of creditor cannot repossess their goods without the consent of the examiner.

Rents and Leases

Rent is often a very significant issue for companies in examinership (especially multi-unit retail companies) and will often be presented in the IER as a key issue to be addressed. The examiner will meet with the landlords and address the main concerns, which usually relate to the level of rent being charged, and the period and conditions of the lease. It is important to note that unless a landlord or lessor consents in writing, the court cannot order a reduction in the amount of rent. Therefore, it is for the examiner to come to an agreement with the landlord in respect of any proposed rent reduction. This must also be considered in terms of the scheme of arrangement whereby such an agreement would affect the landlords right to repossess or other types of reliefs to recover rent.

The 2013 examinership of the *McGovern Group* of companies is a good practical case study of how an examinership can right-size rents for a multi-unit retail business. It involved two trading entities (McGovern Fashions Ltd and Seduzca Ltd) and one holding company (One9 JD Investment Property Holdings Ltd), which was the shareholder for the two trading companies. The trading companies operated seven retail units across Ireland under their own brand name together with four stores operating under the brand 'Jack & Jones'. The companies entered the examinership process in the summer of 2013. The critical issues facing the trading companies were reduction in turnover, caused by a general decline in disposable income, and unsustainable levels of rent paid by their stores. The independent expert was clear in his report when he stated that a condition of the companies' survival was the renegotiation or repudiation of leases in which they entered.

Immediately following his appointment, the examiner contacted each of the companies' landlords in order to update them on developments and seek to hold initial meetings. At the commencement of the examinership period, the companies' total annual rent bill was in the region of €950,000.

During the examinership process the companies closed one store and handed back its lease. This unit was loss making and even on reduced rental terms it would remain so. A repudiation application was not required as the company operating the store had leased it from another company within the wider group not forming part of the examinership process. A fixed-charge receiver was appointed over the assets of this related company and the receiver accepted the handing back of the lease. Following intense negotiations with all of the companies' landlords, the examiner achieved a reduction in annual rental payments in the amount of €296,000 in respect of those stores that would continue to trade, a 38% reduction in contractual rents per annum. The examiner also negotiated a number of rent-free periods in order to allow the companies further breathing space when exiting the examinership process.

The examiner's scheme of arrangement was successfully approved by the company's creditors and the High Court in November 2013, with all companies exiting the examinership process. In total, 31 jobs were saved, including those in the store that was closed during the protection period, as these staff members were re-deployed to other stores.

Debtors

As discussed above in the section about "Monitoring Key Aspects of the Business", it is important that debtors are collected in the normal manner throughout the examinership process so that the company can continue to trade. In reality, the less that customers become involved in the examinership process, the better. It is important that a clear 'business as usual' message goes out to all key customers at a very early stage of the protection period.

Working Capital

It is important that the company seeking the protection of the court is not projected to be trading at a loss through the period of protection. In many recent cases, existing shareholders have provided finance to support the working capital of the company.

If the examiner considers that the company's cash flow is no longer viable, then he or she is obliged to report back to the court so that no further credit is incurred by the company to the detriment of its suppliers.

"In examination under Part 10 of the Companies Act 2014"

Finally, it is important to note that as soon as a company comes under the protection of the court, all invoices, orders for goods, business letters issued, marketing material and the company's website, including electronic mail, must contain the words "in examination under Part 10 of the Companies Act 2014". This has evolved from the original wording "under the protection of the Court" and now if an interim examiner is appointed on the day of the petition, typically correspondence from the company will state clearly "interim examiner appointed", to reflect the fact the full hearing of the petition has not yet taken place. Any person who does not comply with these requirements will be in breach of the Act and subject to a fine.

KEY POINTS: THE ROLE OF THE EXAMINER

1. An examiner will usually meet the directors of the company before the appointment to assess whether it is appropriate for them to consent to act.
2. Once appointed, the examiner will write to creditors, shareholders, directors, the Revenue Commissioners, the company's bank and utility providers to set out the date of appointment, a briefing about the examinership process, contact details and a request to submit any invoices outstanding from before the company entered examinership.
3. During the first week of the examinership, the examiner typically meets with the company's staff, key customers and key suppliers to review the issues that are likely to be critical for a successful examinership.

4. In the early stages of the examinership, the examiner must check that assertions made in the independent expert's report (IER) are factual and ensure that the company does indeed have a reasonable prospect of survival.

5. If the company is not capable of survival, the examiner must ask for court protection to be removed. The company will then be placed in receivership, if a secured creditor decides to appoint a receiver, or the company will be liquidated.

6. The examiner is obliged to deliver a Form E24 (Notice of petition for appointment of examiner) to the Companies Registration Office (CRO) within three days of presenting the petition.

7. The appointment of an examiner should not affect the day-to-day management of the company; however, the examiner is able to preside over board meetings.

8. The examiner must also keep the Office of the Director of Corporate Enforcement informed about developments in the examinership and outline the reasons that the company has entered examinership and the role of directors in that process.

9. The role of the examiner includes monitoring cash flow on a weekly basis and comparing actuals with the cash flow projections outlined in the IER.

10. It is essential that the examiner ensures the company is compliant in filing tax returns and discharging taxes as they fall due.

8.

The Investment Process

- Introduction
- Funding
- The Investment Agreement
- The Escrow Agreement
- Key Points: The Investment Process

Introduction

In order for an examinership to be successful, funding is inevitably going to be required to facilitate the scheme of arrangement, fund the post-examinership strategy and pay the examiner and legal fees arising from the examinership. As referred to throughout this book, this funding is required to be secured during the protection period before the examiner can put forward proposals for a scheme of arrangement between the company, its members and its creditors. Following the appointment of the examiner, in the vast majority of cases, the process of securing investment commences almost immediately. In this chapter, we will set out the types of funding available to a company during examinership and describe the investment process to be undertaken by the examiner.

Funding

An examiner can typically secure funding from one of five sources:
- existing resources of the company;
- re-financing;
- new investors;
- generation of surplus cash flow;
- sale of non-core assets.

Investment from Existing Resources

When a company is in examinership and requires investment to survive, very often the company's incumbent directors, shareholders or management express interest in investing in the company themselves. While such incumbents tend to be well placed to invest, as they have in-depth knowledge of the business, and there is also little or no need for them to carry out due diligence, it is important to note that if a company enters examinership, there can be no guarantee that its incumbent directors, shareholders or management will remain so following the conclusion of the process. The company must be insolvent to be in examinership in the first place and will need funding to survive, even if that means significant changes are necessary to the ownership and governance of the business.

While in certain cases, existing stakeholders may not be in a position to put forward an investment proposal to the examiner, typically the incumbents have identified an investor who is willing to submit an investment proposal on their behalf, which involves the incumbent management remaining in control of day-to-day operations. There is a certain element of continuity to such investment proposals, with retention of key staff often an integral part of ensuring the future viability of the business.

Re-financing

At the time of writing, there remain three pillar banks in Ireland. There have been cases in recent years in which a pillar bank has provided funding to a company as part of an examinership process. The *Kenny Galway Limited* case in 2016 (AIB) and the *Dublin Food Sales Limited* case in 2020 (Bank of Ireland) are both examples of companies being rescued through fresh pillar bank funding. In more recent times, the banks' normal reticence to consider funding companies under the protection of the court has evolved. For this to be considered, a bank will request certain information, including an updated business plan with accompanying trading projections. This is a critical piece of documentation, as it will provide the bank with details of the future plans for the company and, most importantly, its post-examinership repayment capacity in relation to any potential refinancing to be discussed and agreed.

More recent years have seen the emergence in the Irish market of a number of 'challenger banks', providing asset-based lending facilities to companies and showing a willingness to support companies that are undergoing formal restructuring. The most common types of funding offered by these challenger banks involve the provision of funding against assets such as property, plant and machinery, and vehicles, and an invoice-discounting facility in relation to a company's debtor ledger. Invoice discounting is a mechanism whereby a lender will advance immediate cash flow to a company on the basis of a percentage of the value of outstanding customer invoices (debtors). In order to explore the possibility of any such asset-based lending, a company will be required to maintain up-to-date and accurate asset registers and debtor ledgers. While this form of financing is slightly more expensive than conventional pillar bank lending, the willingness of these challenger banks to support formal restructuring and their ability to provide funding within a short timeframe make them a viable possibility for securing fresh finance.

It should be noted these re-financing options are also available to potential external investors, though they are more commonly associated with existing stakeholders.

New Investors

In Ireland, in order to attract and secure external investment, an examiner will typically place an advertisement in a reputable Sunday newspaper immediately following their appointment. The advertisement will outline that the examiner is seeking expressions of interest in investing in the company. An examiner will normally allow a very short window (typically from five days to two weeks) for the receipt of expressions of interest, given the tight timelines they must adhere to in an examination process. In addition to placing an advertisement in the newspaper, an examiner can sometimes also rely on media coverage to attract interested parties, though this is usually only afforded to larger, high-profile companies that have sought the protection of the court.

Furthermore, the company may have been in negotiations with potential investors prior to petitioning for examinership, in which case the examiner will contact these interested parties. The examiner will also speak with the existing stakeholders to ascertain whether there are any other potential interested parties that should be contacted. It is the responsibility of an examiner to provide a return to the creditors of the company at least as positive as they would receive in the event of a winding up, and when an examiner seeks support for the scheme of arrangement presented at the meeting of members and creditors (see Chapter 9), it is important that they can provide assurances that what is being proposed is the best available investment and that all possible avenues have been explored as part of the investment process.

Each interested party that submits an expression of interest to the examiner is required to sign a non-disclosure agreement (NDA) in advance of receiving any information regarding the company under protection of the court. As such information is often commercially sensitive, this is a critical part of any investment process.

Once the required NDAs are in place, each interested party will receive an information memorandum (IM) from the examiner. The IM contains high-level information about the company and sets out the timelines for the submission of investment proposals for consideration by the examiner. The IM is prepared by the examiner's staff in conjunction with the company. It outlines what details and information the examiner requires in respect of any investment proposal that is to be submitted, most commonly including criteria such as:
- details of the proposed investment;
- nature of the proposed investment (debt and/or equity);
- background to the investor(s);

- proof of funding;
- a detailed business plan for the future;
- retention of staff;
- proposed board of directors;
- timelines for completion;
- any conditions attached to the investment proposal;
- due diligence requests.

Following receipt of indicative investment proposals, the examiner will carry out a review of the investment proposals received with a view to inviting one or more interested parties to carry out due diligence on the company. The examiner will consider all of the above criteria in the IM to identify the investment proposal that is best tailored to ensuring the survival of the company in the long run and, in turn, the preservation of employment.

This due diligence process is facilitated by the company and overseen by the examiner and their staff. It involves the collation of all due diligence queries from all remaining interested parties, collating the information and distributing an identical information pack to each potential investor. When this information pack is being distributed, the examiner and their team will communicate the timelines for the submission of final investment proposals for consideration. It is important to note that timelines in respect of an investment process can be altered or amended at the discretion of the examiner, and that certain information requests may be declined if the examiner deems the information sought to be too commercially sensitive. (Mr Justice Brian Cregan referred to the examiner's discretion in relation to the investment process in his judgment in the 2015 *Ladbrokes* examinership – see further below.)

During the due diligence phase, it is common for an examiner to seek a meeting with each of the remaining interested parties. These meetings provide the examiner with a greater understanding of the background to each of the potential investors, their trading history, plans for the business and, importantly, their ability to execute an investment agreement should they be selected as the preferred investor. It also provides each interested party with an opportunity to discuss various aspects of the process with the examiner, as it may be the first time the potential investor has been involved in an examination process.

Upon receipt of final investment proposals from the remaining interested parties, the examiner will carefully review and consider the content of each investment proposal received. This review is usually undertaken with the assistance of the examiner's legal advisors. It is important to note that the investment process in an examinership is not simply 'a bidding war' with preferred investor status being awarded to the highest bidder. The examiner will carefully consider a number of factors in respect of any investment proposal received, as outlined in the list above. In addition to the risk that a proposed investor may not be in a position to complete their investment, at the forefront of the examiner's consideration will be the investor's plans regarding existing employees of the company. For example, an interested party may be proposing by far the largest investment sum but may not have any plans to retain the existing staff. In such an instance, the examiner cannot consider the investment proposal as this goes against a core principle of the examinership process, i.e. employment protection.

The examiner will also consider a potential investor's business plan for the company, including a review of the investor's trading projections. Significant emphasis will be placed on future projections to ensure that the company has a reasonable prospect of survival, a critical condition the court must also be satisfied has been met in order to approve any scheme or arrangement that is formulated.

In addition, a post-examinership balance sheet will be prepared, projecting the financial position of a company after it exits the process. One of the main benefits of examinership is the generation of a 'clean' balance sheet for the company following its restructuring as a result of the removal of historical debt in accordance with the terms of the formulated scheme of arrangement (see Chapter 9). An examiner will review the projected post-examinership balance sheet included in a proposed investment, particularly key factors such as the working capital ratio, in order to ensure that the company stands a reasonable prospect of survival with that investor.

As mentioned above, Mr Justice Cregan outlined in his *Ladbrokes* judgment that the selection of a preferred investor is at the discretion of the examiner based on their professional, commercial judgement, and within the requirements of the legislation (e.g. that the protection of employment is paramount). This discretion is exercised following a detailed review of the final investment proposals received. The *Ladbrokes* decision followed the earlier similar 2012 decision of Mr Justice Kelly in the *Eircom* case. Unless the examiner acts in an absurd manner, the court will not interfere in the selection of the preferred investor.

When the examiner has selected a preferred investment proposal, the investor will be notified and afforded a period of exclusivity. During this period, the investor will carry out any remaining due diligence that may be required for their final proposal. The investor will also ensure that the investment funds are readily available to be transferred to the nominated escrow account (as described below). This is a critical part of the process. If it becomes apparent during this period of exclusivity that there are doubts surrounding the investor's ability to transfer the investment sum, the examiner must consider whether to return to an alternative interested party to ascertain whether they remain interested in investing. It is for this reason that a period of exclusivity tends to be relatively short. Given the tight timelines involved in an examinership process, an examiner must be satisfied and certain that the selected investor can execute an investment agreement within the agreed timelines. Any uncertainty at this stage of the process will negatively affect the examiner's willingness to proceed any further with the selected investor. It is also for this reason that it is far more advantageous for an examiner to have a number of external interested parties remaining in the process for as long as possible.

Generation of Surplus Cash Flow

An alternative potential source of funding is from the generation of surplus cash flow during the protection period. While this is more likely in a cash-driven seasonal business, it is not a common source of funding in an examinership due to the fact that companies that enter the examination process tend to see their credit terms limited or removed completely by suppliers, and there is often a requirement to pay cash on delivery for any orders placed during the protection period. In addition, a company exiting the examination process will require working capital in order to trade and an investor will more often than not prefer not to risk starving the company of cash reserves.

While uncommon, however, there have been cases where the investment sourced to formulate a scheme of arrangement has consisted of company funds generated from surplus cash flow, such as in the 2012 examinership of the *Deerhaven Group*, a greeting card chain that used funds from its busiest period of the year to fund the examiner's scheme. In situations where cash flow is used in this way, an examiner must be satisfied that the company will have the ability to trade going forward and pay its debts as they fall due. This can be achieved in a number of ways. First, the examiner will scrutinise the future cash-flow projections to ascertain the company's ability to continue to trade. In addition, the examiner will typically look for an undertaking from the selected investor to provide additional working capital to the company if and when it is required. He or she will seek written confirmation of this undertaking, together with proof of funding for any necessary additional working capital. This will then be exhibited to the court during the hearing for the confirmation of the scheme of arrangement (the 'confirmation hearing') in order to provide the court with additional assurance in relation to a company's reasonable prospect of survival (see Chapter 9).

Sale of Non-core Assets

The sale of non-core company assets is also a potential source of funding for a scheme of arrangement. However, as with the generation of surplus cash, this option is less common than sourcing investment through existing or new investors; often, many of the non-core assets will have been disposed of in advance of a company seeking the protection of the court in order to pay creditors. There are also risks attached to relying solely on the disposal of non-core assets to fund a scheme of arrangement given the uncertainty of the value of any realisations due to the perceived forced sale nature of the disposal. However, as with the generation of surplus cash flow, disposal of non-core assets can and has been used in a number of examinerships as part of the process to secure scheme funding.

If a company is in possession of non-core assets that are available for immediate disposal, there are a number of steps that must be followed prior to any potential disposal. First, the examiner must be provided with evidence that the assets in question are unencumbered, meaning that they are owned outright by the company and not subject to any charge registered in favour of a secured creditor. Upon receipt of documentary evidence confirming unencumbered ownership, the examiner will also seek assurances that the assets are in fact non-core assets and that the business of the company will not be negatively impacted by selling the assets in question.

In addition, the examiner must consider the likelihood that the identified assets will be disposed of within a short period of time, taking into account the strict timelines of the examinership process. A professional valuation of such assets is also required in order to ascertain the level of potential funding that may become available from their sale. Once the above steps have been taken, the examiner can instruct the company to dispose of the non-core assets. As we have seen in the previous chapter, executive powers tend to remain with the company's directors in examinerships and, typically, an examiner would not have the power to dispose of a non-core company asset but rather would advise the company on any such disposal.

This form of funding for a scheme of arrangement is also commonly used to settle secured creditor claims against the company. The examiner's scheme can provide for non-core assets to be disposed of, with the full proceeds to be paid to the secured creditor, often in full settlement of the secured claim.

The Investment Agreement

Once the examiner is satisfied that an appropriate source of funding has been identified, there are a number of documents that will need to be executed in advance of convening the members' and creditors' meetings (see Chapter 9). It is at this stage of the process that legal advisors take on a more prominent role as they are tasked with settling these documents on behalf on the examiner and the investor. The investment agreement is required to be executed in advance of convening the meetings of the members and creditors. It sets out the quantum of the sum being invested, together with any terms and conditions attached to the investment. A copy of the formulated scheme of arrangement will also be appended to the investment agreement.

The Escrow Agreement

As mentioned above, transferring the investment sum to a nominated escrow account is a critical part of the investment process. An escrow agreement is an agreement by the investor to transfer the investment sum to a third party (an 'escrow agent'), usually the legal advisors of the examiner. The escrow agreement will contain details of the quantum of funds to be transferred and the conditions governing release of the funds from the escrow agent. The agreement, once settled, is executed between the investor and the escrow agent. The funds are then held by the escrow agent until predetermined contractual obligations have been fulfilled or appropriate instructions received.

Upon approval of the scheme of arrangement by the court and when any other predetermined conditions have been fulfilled, the funds held by the escrow agent are released to the company, minus any professional fees incurred. The funds are then used by the company to distribute the relevant dividends in accordance with the approved scheme of arrangement (see Chapter 9). Should the proposed scheme of arrangement be rejected by the court, the escrow agreement will stipulate that the funds are immediately released back to the investor's nominated bank account. The court will often seek a copy of the executed investment agreement and related escrow agreements as part of the consideration to approve a scheme of arrangement formulated by an examiner.

KEY POINTS: THE INVESTMENT PROCESS

1. Investment in a company in examinership is pivotal, as financial backing is required to cover the money owed to creditors, fund the post-examinership strategy and pay the professional fees of the examinership.
2. Examiners can secure funding from existing sources, re-financing, new investors, surplus cash flow and the sale of non-core assets.
3. Incumbent directors, shareholders or management tend to be well placed to invest as they have in-depth knowledge of the company and there is little need for them to carry out due diligence.
4. Banks have been known to provide funding to companies undergoing formal restructuring if they can provide an updated business plan with trading projections and detailing future plans and the capacity to repay potential refinancing.
5. In order to attract new external investment, an examiner will typically place an advertisement in the *Sunday Business Post* seeking expressions of interest in the company.
6. Once a non-disclosure agreement (NDA) is in place, an information memorandum will be issued to interested parties containing high-level information about the company and the timelines for submission of investment proposals.
7. Investment proposals typically include the details and nature of the proposed investment, the investor's background, proof of funding, proposed board of directors, additional due diligence requests and conditions attached to the proposal. These proposals will be reviewed by the examiner and invites will be sent to interested parties to carry out due diligence on the company.
8. Due diligence queries will be answered, and information is compiled into an identical document sent to each potential investor. Parties who are still interested will provide final investment proposals to be reviewed by the examiner who will consider their business plans, especially plans for maintaining employment.
9. The examiner will also review the projected post-examinership balance sheet, especially the working capital ratio, to ensure that the company stands a reasonable prospect of survival. The process of selecting a preferred investor is at the discretion of the examiner based on professional judgement and subject to the requirements of the legislation.

10. If the company decides to sell non-core assets, the examiner must be provided with evidence that the assets are owned outright by the company and that the selling of these assets will not have a negative impact on the business.
11. An investment agreement is required to set out the quantum of the sum being invested, with any terms and conditions attached to the investment.
12. The investment sum is then transferred to an escrow agent, and an agreement will contain details of the funds to be transferred and the conditions governing the release of these funds.
13. Upon approval of the scheme of arrangement by the court and the fulfilment of any other predetermined conditions, the funds will be released from escrow to the company, minus any professional fees incurred.

9.

The Scheme of Arrangement

- Introduction
- What is a Scheme of Arrangement?
- Members' and Creditors' Meetings
- Submission of the Scheme to the Court for Approval
- Rejection of a Scheme of Arrangement
- Opposition to a Scheme of Arrangement
- Implementation of a Scheme of Arrangement
- Key Points: The Scheme of Arrangement

Introduction

Throughout this book there have been many references to the 'proposal for a compromise' or the 'scheme of arrangement'. In this chapter we will explain what a scheme of arrangement is and its purpose. We will also discuss the members' and creditors' meetings convened by the examiner at the end of the examinership in order to allow these key stakeholders to vote on the scheme of arrangement that the examiner is proposing, how the scheme of arrangement is submitted to the court for approval, the types of objections that can be raised by members and creditors to a scheme of arrangement, and the practical steps required to implement a scheme of arrangement once it has been approved.

What is a Scheme of Arrangement?

The scheme of arrangement, also known as the 'proposal for compromise', is the ultimate objective of the examinership process and is formulated by the examiner once they have carried out their duties (see Chapter 7) and finalised the investment process (see Chapter 8). The 'scheme' sets out how the company will emerge from examinership, detailing the sum being used to facilitate the exit and the dividends payable to all classes of creditors in respect of liabilities up to the date of the successful petition for examinership. The scheme of arrangement is a legally binding document and, if approved by the court, is enforceable on all members and creditors of the company. The purpose of the scheme is to allow for the survival of the company, *not* for a break-up or disposal of the company's assets. Therefore, the scheme must provide for the survival of the corporate entity, not just the survival of the underlying business.

In accordance with the legislation, the scheme of arrangement must include the following features:

• The scheme specifies each class of member and creditor of the company. The types of member may include ordinary or preference shareholders. The list of members will set out the shareholding of each member. The creditors of the company will be listed in accordance with their security and order of priority as set out in the legislation. As we have seen in Chapter 5, a company's creditors are usually comprised of secured creditors, leasing creditors, super-preferential creditors, preferential creditors, unsecured creditors and connected creditors. The list of creditors included in the scheme will set out the balance owed to each creditor at the petition date.

- The scheme specifies any class of member and/or creditor whose interests or claims will be impaired by the scheme. A member's interests are impaired if the nominal value of their shareholding is reduced, or amount of fixed dividend is reduced, or they are deprived of any rights accruing to them, or their percentage of overall shareholding is reduced, or they are deprived of their shareholding in the company. A creditor's claim is impaired if they are receiving less than its full amount or over a longer time frame than originally contracted.
- The scheme must provide for equal treatment of each interest or claim of a particular class of member or creditor, unless they agree to accept a lesser treatment. For example, all unsecured creditors must receive the same dividend and the examiner may not prefer one unsecured creditor over the general body of creditors in that class.
- The scheme sets out the dividend payable to each class of creditor. In most cases, a class of creditor will only receive a percentage dividend on the amount owed to them. Secured creditors will receive a dividend equal to the market value of their security or their full balance due will be restructured over a period of time. However, the examiner can also propose an additional amount, for example one that is likely to be collected by the company in the future, to be set aside to pay an additional dividend to all creditors within a particular class on a pro-rata basis. For example, in the 2013 examinership of *SIAC Construction Limited*, the examiner formulated a scheme where all creditors, with the exception of secured creditors, bank and inter-company creditors, would receive an additional 20% dividend, on a pro-rata basis, resulting from any realisations arising from a legal action being taken by the company in another jurisdiction.
- The scheme sets out any changes to the management or board of directors of the company if the examiner determines it is desirable to do so in order to facilitate the survival of the company. In many cases, there are deficiencies within existing management and/or the board and the examiner will recommend the appointment of an additional director with relevant industry experience in order to facilitate the survival of the company after it exits examinership.
- The scheme specifies any changes the examiner recommends be made to the constitution of the company. The most common change to company constitutions recommended by examiners is to increase the authorised share capital as a result of the investment in the company through the investment process. This ensures that the company is sufficiently capitalised post examinership.
- The scheme includes a statement of the assets and liabilities of the company at the date the scheme is proposed, showing both the position of the company operating as a going concern and the

subsequent position on a winding-up basis, if the company were to be liquidated.

As mentioned in Chapter 7, though the examiner is required to return to court before or on Day 70 of the protection period with a proposed scheme of arrangement, in most cases the examiner will not be in a position to issue a scheme of arrangement before or on Day 70, but will expect to do so once the investment process is finalised (see Chapter 8). In such cases, the examiner must report back to the court on or before Day 70 and the court will grant the examiner an extension up to Day 100 of the protection period if the examiner is satisfied, and has provided sufficient evidence to the court, that they will be in a position to formulate and issue a scheme of arrangement.

There have been a number of cases in which the examiner has issued schemes and held creditor meetings before reaching Day 70. For example, in the 2012 examinership of *Eircom*, a formerly state-owned telecommunications operator, and in the 2018 *Frontier Entertainment Limited* examinership, an operator of the tourist attraction site The Vaults in Dublin's city centre, the examiners' schemes of arrangement were confirmed by the court on Day 54 and Day 37 of the protection period respectively, following a swift conclusion of the investment process.

Working back, if the examiner is going to conclude the examinership process within the 100-day timeframe, they are required to send the proposals to all members and creditors no later than Day 96 of the protection period, provided that the remaining four days of the protection period are working days. The examiner is required to provide three clear days' notice, which does not include weekends or public holidays, to all members and creditors in respect of the meetings to be held. The examiner must then report back to the court no later than Day 100 of the protection period on the outcome of the members' and creditors' meetings held for the purposes of voting on the scheme of arrangement prepared by the examiner.

In some examinerships, a modified scheme of arrangement is prepared between issuing the scheme of arrangement to the members and creditors and the holding of meetings with them. These modifications usually include changes to creditors' names or their balances, or wording to a specific section of the scheme at the request of a creditor. These modifications are then put before the members and creditors at their meetings to vote on. If approved by the members and creditors, the modified scheme of arrangement is also presented to the court for approval.

Finally, with regard to liabilities, any liabilities incurred by the company after the successful presentation of the petition to appoint an examiner do not form part of the scheme of arrangement. Any post-petition liabilities should be paid by the company within the credit terms provided by the supplier.

Members' and Creditors' Meetings

As mentioned above, after the examiner has issued their scheme of arrangement to the members and creditors of the company, meetings are convened with these parties in order to allow the members and creditors to vote on the scheme. As examinership is a court-led process, the holding and convening of these meetings should be in accordance with the Rules of the Superior Courts.

The examiner presides as the chair of all meetings of members and creditors that are convened and is required to conduct the meetings in an orderly manner. The members' meetings are held first and then the creditors by class. At these meetings, the examiner will provide a brief summary of the effect of the proposed scheme of arrangement on the class of member or creditor present, including any modifications to the scheme of arrangement. It is also the responsibility of the examiner to allow sufficient time for queries from the members and creditors on the scheme of arrangement and for a proper discussion with all present. The examiner will also read out the results from any other meetings held earlier in the day, if requested to do so.

The Rules of the Superior Courts and the legislation do not state whether the examiner has to be physically present to chair meetings of members and creditors. In the 2017 examinership of *FCR Media Limited* (the company behind Golden Pages), the examiner was overseas at the time the meetings were held. The meetings were conducted via Skype with prior consent from the major creditors of the company for the meetings to be held in this way.

Notices of Meetings and Accompanying Documents

The examiner is responsible for convening all meetings of members and creditors. These meetings are convened by the examiner by issuing notices by post to all members and creditors together not less than three days before the date of the meeting. If a member or creditor is in more than one class, they should receive a notice for the meeting of each class that they are in. The notice issued to members and creditors will contain the details of the meetings, including the date, time and location. The notice issued to each creditor or member is sent to the address known to the examiner. In practice, notices of meetings are also sent by email, where email addresses are available, to all members and creditors of the company. This is particularly relevant for creditors or members who reside overseas, given the short notice and practical challenges of attending the meetings.

The previous legislation did not exclude weekends or public holidays from the three-day rule. However, the Companies Act 2014 clearly states that "Where in this Act anything is required or allowed to be done within a number of days not exceeding 6, a day that is a Saturday, a Sunday or a public holiday shall not be reckoned in computing that number". This is also re-enforced by the Rules of Superior Courts. In addition, the day of a meeting of members or creditors is not considered as a day for the purposes of calculating the three clear days. For example, if the meeting of members and creditors were to be held on a Monday, the notices together with all other paperwork (discussed below) would be required to be issued on the Tuesday of the previous week in order to allow three clear days, being Wednesday, Thursday and Friday.

The following documents should accompany the notices issued in respect of the members' and creditors' meetings:
• general and special proxy forms that are used to appoint an individual to appear on a member's or creditor's behalf;
• a copy of the proposed scheme of arrangement; and
• an explanatory memorandum explaining the effect of the scheme on the company's members and creditors.

These documents should also be included in emails sent to members and creditors regarding the meeting. Subsequently, an affidavit (referred to as the 'affidavit of service') will be prepared and filed by the examiner, the examiner's solicitor or a member of the examiner's staff, with the court prior to the confirmation hearing. The affidavit states that the above-mentioned documents have been posted to all members and creditors in accordance with the Rules of the Superior Courts and the legislation. The court accepts this affidavit as sufficient evidence of notice having been appropriately issued to all members and creditors of the company.

The Location of Meetings

The examiner will convene meetings in a location that is convenient for the majority of members and creditors. In practice, the examiner will review the registered addresses of the company's creditors and decide on the most suitable location and time to allow members and creditors the opportunity to attend the meetings.

Voting

Upon answering any queries from members and creditors present at their respective meetings, the examiner will request all present to vote for or against the proposed scheme of arrangement. Ballot papers are handed out to all present, which are then collected and counted by the examiner. The examiner also casts the votes of those members and creditors that have appointed them as their proxy (see below). All votes are tallied and the results are then confirmed at the meeting. In order for a scheme of arrangement to be approved by a class of member or creditor, the majority of the class that have participated in the meeting must vote in favour of the scheme in number (i.e. a simple majority) and value of balances due. In accordance with the legalisation, the scheme of arrangement must be accepted by one class of impaired creditor in order to allow the examiner to return to the court and seek its confirmation of the scheme of arrangement. Therefore, the creditors can effectively veto the scheme, if they act collectively.

Voting by Proxy

Each member and creditor of the company is entitled to attend and vote at the meetings convened by the examiner. Members and creditors can vote at a meeting by either attending in person or submitting a completed proxy form to the examiner prior to the meeting. (A proxy allows a party to vote at a meeting even though they are unable to attend in person.) There are a number of parties that a member or creditor can appoint as their proxy to vote at a members' or creditors' meeting, including the chair of the meeting, i.e. the examiner, or commonly the member's or creditor's solicitor or accountant. By default, when acting as proxy for a member or creditor, the examiner will vote in favour of the scheme of arrangement, unless it is stated otherwise on the proxy form.

Where a proxy is submitted by an incorporated entity, it should be duly signed by an authorised officer of that entity in order to ensure that the vote is valid at the relevant meeting. It is at the discretion of the examiner to decide whether a proxy form is validly completed and if the vote by proxy should be allowed. In order for a proxy form to be accepted by the examiner and admitted for voting at the relevant meeting, it should be lodged with the examiner no later than 4 pm on the day preceding the meeting in question. The examiner should have all relevant and completed proxy forms available at each meeting for inspection by any party.

In many cases, individuals representing creditor companies attend meetings without first submitting a completed proxy form to the examiner. If the creditor is a sole trader, then he or she can still vote at the meeting. However, as set out above, where the creditor is a company, it must have submitted a proxy appointing a person to vote on its behalf. It is at the examiner's discretion whether to allow or disallow a vote from anyone who has not been validly appointed. While the examiner can allow this party to vote, their vote will not be counted in the overall total in respect of approving the proposed scheme of arrangement. In the examiner's report to the court, it will be noted that a member or creditor voted, but their vote was not counted as it was considered invalid.

Examples of where this can occur include where a creditor has not submitted a proxy form to the examiner within the specified timeframe, but still attends the meeting in order to vote, or where a creditor disputes their inclusion in a particular class of creditors and attends the meeting of the class of creditors in which they feel they should be included. It will be explained to the creditor that, while they can still vote, their vote is not valid and will not be included in the final count for that particular class, though it will be included in the examiner's report to the court how the creditor voted.

Quorate Requirements

In order for a meeting to be quorate (meaning that a sufficient number of parties are in attendance at the meeting as prescribed in the legislation), at least three creditors of the company that are entitled to vote at the meetings must be present or represented. In the case of members, at least two members should be present or represented at their meetings. In practice, the majority of members and creditors attend their meeting by proxy, with either the examiner appointed as their proxy or a third party representing them (see above).

If a quorum is not present at the meetings, the examiner is required, in accordance with the Rules of the Superior Courts, to reconvene the meetings of members and creditors. Though adjourned for seven days, the meetings are held at the same time and place as originally set out in the notice. However, this often creates practical issues for the examiner because, as we have seen above, the period of protection is only for 100 days and the examiner is required to present the results of the member and creditor meetings to the court within the 100-day timeframe.

Therefore, it is often difficult for the examiner to adjourn members' and creditors' meetings, as most of such meetings are not held until the latter days of the examinership and it may not be feasible for the examiner to reconvene meetings if there was no quorum present. For example, the Revenue Commissioners is a separate class of creditor (a 'super preferential creditor'), in respect of employee PRSI deductions. As there is only ever one creditor in this class, the examiner will never be in a position to meet the quorum. In this scenario, the examiner seeks permission from the court to dispense with the requirement to reconvene meetings for the relevant class of creditor where no quorum was present.

Other Matters

The examiner should also ensure that:
- minutes of members' and creditors' meetings are kept and entered into the minutes of the company;
- the minutes are signed by the examiner; and
- a list of members and creditors that attended the meetings is kept.

Submission of the Scheme to the Court for Approval

Following the convening and holding of the meetings of members and creditors, the examiner is required to prepare a report on the outcome of the meetings and submit it to the court. This is referred to as the *'examiner's report'* in the legislation. Once it has heard the application to consider the examiner's report, the court can confirm the proposed scheme of arrangement, refuse confirmation of the proposals or approve the proposals subject to whatever modifications it considers necessary.

As we have seen in Chapter 7, where the examiner is unable to formulate proposals for a compromise or scheme of arrangement within the 70-day limit, they may apply to the court for an extension of time, not exceeding 30 days, which the court will grant if satisfied that the extension of time is required in order to formulate a scheme of arrangement and present same to the members and creditors of the company.

The Examiner's Report

The legislation is prescriptive about the contents of the examiner's report. It must include:
- A copy of the scheme of arrangement placed before the meetings of members and creditors.
- Details of any modifications to the scheme of arrangement by members and creditors at the meetings, which are usually set out in the modified proposals appended to the report.
- The voting outcome of the meetings, detailing all members and creditors who voted on the proposals.
- The recommendation of a creditor's committee of inspection, if any was appointed. (In practice, creditor's committees are seldom, if ever, seen in examinership cases and are far more common in liquidations.)
- A statement of the assets and liabilities of the company at the date of the examiner's report, as set out in the scheme of arrangement.
- A list of all creditors of the company, the amount owing to each creditor, and the nature and value of any security held by any creditor, which, again, is as set out in the scheme of arrangement.
- A list of the directors and other officers of the company.
- The examiner's recommendation to the court to confirm the proposals.
- Any such matters as the examiner deems appropriate.

This last requirement, "any such matters as the examiner deems appropriate", is where the examiner has discretion to include information they believe is relevant to assist the court in making its decision to approve the scheme of arrangement. Such information would include details on how the company has traded during the protection period, future trading projections to demonstrate how it can survive as a going concern (see Chapter 5), details of the investment process undertaken (see Chapter 8), any issues that have arisen during the protection period and details of any changes to the management of the company.

Projections

It is essential for the examiner to include trading or cash-flow projections for the company for the first 12 months after it exits examinership. This will demonstrate to the court (and to creditors) that the company can survive once it has been restructured through the examinership process and the timeframe of 12 months is consistent with the accounting concept of 'going concern'. Working with the company's management, the examiner should scrutinise these projections and provide an opinion to the court as to whether they consider that the projections are reasonable and attainable.

As well as the court, the examiner must also serve their report on the company itself, any notice party to the proceedings, any creditor objecting to the scheme and any other party as directed to by the court.

The Confirmation Hearing

Once the examiner has submitted their report to the court, the court will then set a hearing date for the purposes of confirming the examiner's scheme of arrangement, i.e. the *confirmation hearing*. As discussed above, in most examinerships, the examiner's report is not submitted to the court until Day 100 or a few days prior to Day 100. To this end, the court will set the confirmation hearing for a date following Day 100, as it may not be in a position to hear the examiner's application on the day they present their report; therefore, the court extends its protection up to the date of the confirmation hearing beyond Day 100. The length of the extended period of protection beyond Day 100 will depend on the level of objection from members and/or creditors of the company to the examiner's scheme of arrangement. If there is no objection from any party, the confirmation hearing will take place, depending on the court's availability, two to three days following the filing of the examiner's report. Should there be an objection from members or creditors, the court, the examiner and the objecting parties will agree a timeline for the exchange of affidavits, with the confirmation hearing usually set for a date within a period of two weeks from the date the examiner files their report. (The types of objection that can be made by members and creditors are discussed in the next section.)

Extensions Beyond Day 100

When extending the period of protection beyond Day 100, the court is conscious that the company will wish to exit the examinership process as quickly as possible and return to normal trading conditions, as the longer its remains in examinership, the more uncertainty over the company's future will continue to grow in the marketplace. For example, a prolonged examinership of a hotel could damage its goodwill, as customers will be concerned that a risk exists that the company may not be in a position to honour its future bookings.

The extended protection period can be *further* extended beyond this two-week period for a number of reasons, two of the most common reasons being:

- the court, due to its own schedule, not sitting and therefore not being available at the time; or
- an objecting member or creditor appealing the court's decision to a higher court.

The issue of court sittings and dates is particularly relevant for the Circuit Court during the vacation sittings, during which the court may only sit once a week and possibly in different locations each time. In the 2017 case of *Com-Plas Packaging Limited and Scriptdale Trading Limited*, which was a Circuit Court examinership, the meetings of members and creditors were held on 27 July 2017, being Day 99 of the examinership, and the examiner's report filed with the Circuit Court later that day. The confirmation hearing did not take place until 7 September 2017, 43 days after the examiner's report was filed with the court and therefore Day 141 of the examinership period. This was as a result of the Circuit Court not sitting during these periods, objections raised by a secured creditor and judge not being available to hear the matter. The court delivered its decision on 12 September 2017, Day 146 of the protection period, approving the examiner's scheme of arrangement. Following this decision, the secured creditor appealed the Circuit Court's decision to the High Court. The examinership eventually concluded on Day 177 of the protection. This demonstrates how the protection period can be extended beyond Day 100 as a result of delays in the judicial system and appeals from objecting parties.

Shareholders' Objections

Members of the company can also object to the examiner's scheme of arrangement, though they do not have a veto in respect of the examiner's proposals and the court will give little weight to a shareholder's objection if they will receive nothing on a winding up of the company. Between 1990 and 1999, the members/shareholders of a company could collectively veto an examiner's scheme of arrangement, essentially leading to scenarios in which the examiner could not prepare a scheme of arrangement where the existing management and members were not the preferred investor of the examiner. This veto was removed by the Companies (Amendment) (No. 2) Act 1999. The court may therefore approve a scheme where the members do not support the examiner's proposals, as was seen in the 2017 case of *Edward Holdings Group*.

Rejection of a Scheme of Arrangement

Where the examiner's scheme of arrangement is rejected by the court, court protection immediately ceases. As the company is insolvent, which, as discussed in Chapter 4, is a prerequisite for seeking the appointment of an examiner, a receiver may be appointed to the company by its secured creditors, an official liquidator may be appointed by the court or a meeting of creditors may be convened by the directors and shareholders in order to appoint a voluntary liquidator.

As the Circuit Court does not have the jurisdiction to appoint a liquidator, this has created some procedural issues in relation to Circuit Court examinerships. In the 2016 examinership of *CS Distributors Limited*, at the confirmation hearing held on 15 June 2016, the Circuit Court did not confirm the examiner's proposals, meaning that the directors were required to make an application to the High Court on 22 June 2016 to seek the appointment of an official liquidator to the company. A similar situation arose in the 2014 Circuit Court examinership of *Copper Bar and Grill Ltd,* where the examiner was not in a position to formulate a scheme of arrangement and therefore applied to the court in order to be discharged as examiner and to remove court protection from the company. A meeting of creditors for the purpose of a voluntary liquidation was held a number of weeks following the removal of court protection.

Reasonable Prospect of Survival

The court will not approve the examiner's proposals unless it is satisfied that the company has a 'reasonable prospect of survival'. (In addition, the court will not approve proposals if the primary purpose is the avoidance of tax.) While, as discussed in Chapter 4, the 'reasonable prospect of survival' issue is mainly dealt with by the court when assessing whether to appoint an examiner in the first instance, it also comes into focus a second time when the court is being asked to approve the examiner's scheme. The court must be satisfied that the company has a reasonable prospect of survival in order to approve the proposals. The purpose of the proposals cannot be to conduct an orderly wind-down of operations. As mentioned above, the evidence to be put before the court to demonstrate this is typically trading or cash-flow projections for a period of at least 12 months. A company can be loss-making for a short time before reverting to profit and this would not alone result in a failure to meet this test if the company can demonstrate that it will remain sufficiently cash-flow positive to discharge its debts as they fall due. Letters of support from customers and creditors would also add to the company's prospects of survival. Projections should also be stress-tested for reasonableness.

Opposition to a Scheme of Arrangement

The Unfair Prejudice Test

As discussed above, a creditor or member may oppose approval of the examiner's proposals. However, the bases on which such parties may oppose the approval of schemes of arrangement are quite narrow:

1. the treatment of a certain member or creditor is unfair when compared with the treatment of other members or creditors in the same class (i.e. are they being treated fairly when compared with how equivalent members or creditors are being treated?); or
2. the treatment of a certain member of creditor is unfair when compared with how they would likely have fared from the outcome of a liquidation or receivership (i.e. are they receiving at least as much as they would in a liquidation or receivership?).

In relation to point 1, if an unsecured creditor is receiving a lower percentage than, for example, another unsecured creditor (e.g. a landlord) then this may be deemed to be unfair.

In relation to point 2, if, for example, a party will recover, say, 40% on a liquidation or receivership, then as a rule, it must secure a return of at least this level under any proposals formulated by the examiner so that they are not unfairly prejudiced.

Other Bases for Opposition

The Companies Act 2014 provides for other bases of opposition to a scheme of arrangement (i.e. other than unfair prejudice) as follows:

- Consent could have been improperly obtained from a creditor at a creditors' meeting. In practice, it is difficult to establish what constitutes 'improperly' in this context. While the examiner must present the proposals clearly and in a way that any class of creditor can understand, it is advisable that any creditor provided with proposals obtains legal advice about their contents. An objection to the proposals will not be accepted simply because a creditor has failed to understand them. However, in practice, claiming that they have been misled by the examiner is not a basis on which creditors object to a scheme of arrangement.

- An objection may be raised if there appears to be some material irregularity at, or in relation to, the meeting at which the proposals are presented. This type of material irregularity would include failure to include a particular class of creditor in the proposals or improper voting at the meeting.

Where the court upholds an objection under the Companies Act, it may make such an order as it deems fit, including:
- an order that the decision of any meeting be set aside; and
- an order that any meeting be reconvened.

Examinerships often result in opposition from various members and creditors. Below are brief synopses of cases involving opposition.

Secured Creditor Opposition

A secured creditor will invariably seek to protect their security and maximise their return. The court will give due regard to the manner in which the secured creditor is being treated in the proposals and particularly if they are being unfairly prejudiced (see above). The following are some examples of how a secured creditor involved in an examinership process may oppose a scheme of arrangement.

In the 2009 case involving *Tivway Limited* and its parent companies, one of their creditors, ACC Bank Plc, appealed the proposed schemes of arrangement formulated by the examiner to the Supreme Court on the basis that they were designed to facilitate the sale of only the profitable assets. It was argued that these schemes were not fulfilling the purpose of an examinership, i.e. to ensure that company survived as a going concern. The Supreme Court allowed the appeal and refused to confirm the proposed schemes of arrangement. The fundamental importance of the reasonable prospect of survival of the company (group) to the entire examinership process was emphasised. Though the sale of the assets laid out in this scheme provided for the survival of the companies, it planned to put the companies into a holding pattern for 10 years. This did not meet the requirement of the legislation that the companies survive as going concerns.

In a Circuit Court examinership in 2017, involving *Com-Plas Packaging Ltd and Scriptdale Trading Ltd* ('*Com-Plas Packaging/Scriptdale Trading*'), a secured creditor, Ennis Property Finance Dac, objected to the proposals formulated, which provided for a write-down of its secured debt.

At the confirmation hearing, Judge Ní Chúlacháin delivered an *ex tempore* judgment in which she approved the proposals as formulated by the examiner and dealt with each point of objection raised by the secured creditor. The objections included the fact that Scriptdale Trading would not have a trading business going forward and that the secured creditor's property rights were being infringed. The judge found that Scriptdale Trading was a going concern, that it was going to be a landlord and, as that was its business, this constituted an undertaking capable of survival.

In relation to the jurisdiction of the Circuit Court to infringe on property rights held by the secured creditor, Judge Ní Chúlacháin found that the examinership legislation provided for interference with property rights and there was nothing untoward in doing so under the proposals, which provided for a splitting of the property (the subject of their security) and the writing down of the secured debt.

With regard to possible unfair prejudice (see above), the valuations provided by a local auctioneer firm, and on which the modified proposals were prepared, were not disputed at any stage by the secured creditor. Although the *Com-Plas Packaging/Scriptdale Trading* scheme of arrangement was ultimately not implemented, it is an important precedent in relation to the Circuit Court's power to write down secured debt.

In the 2011 examinership of *McInerney Homes*, the court determined that it was not appropriate to confirm the scheme of arrangement proposed by the examiner because the scheme was unfairly prejudicial to the interests of a syndicate of McInerney Homes' secured creditors, consisting of Anglo Irish Bank, Bank of Ireland and KBC Bank (the 'banking syndicate'). This case was reopened for the reason that it was highly likely that the interests of two of the banks in loans they had advanced to the applicant and associated companies (McInerney Homes) would be transferred to NAMA, a significantly material fact in considering whether the scheme was unfairly prejudicial to the banking syndicate. The material evidence upon which the new claim was based only became known in the days following the judgment in the case. The court allowed the matter to be reopened on the basis that the transfer of the loans to NAMA could have had a strong bearing on the outcome of the case. In any event, the proposed schemes of arrangement were refused after the case was reopened.

Leasing Creditor Opposition

In the recession that followed the financial crisis of 2008–2009, it was evident that companies (predominantly in the retail sector) were unable to discharge their obligations to landlords under 'upwards only' rent clauses in leases. The Companies Act specifically prohibits a scheme of arrangement that proposes a reduction in future rent or disallows a landlord from enforcing their rights as owners of the property. Furthermore, examinership cannot be used to permit a wholesale repudiation of leases, as demonstrated in the decision of Mr Justice Ryan in *O'Brien's Irish Sandwich Bars Limited*, a 2009 examinership case, and the 2020 decision of Mr Justice McDonald in the examinership of the UK-owned retail chain *New Look Retailers (Ireland) Limited*.

However, nothing prohibits the examiner from negotiating rental terms prior to the proposed scheme of arrangement being presented to a meeting of creditors and at the confirmation hearing. An examiner or a company can apply to the High Court to repudiate contracts (leases) prior to the proposals being formalised and approved by the court, and is therefore in a powerful position when it comes to dealing with landlords of over rented units. This is clear from the decisions of the Supreme Court in the 2010 case *Linen Supply of Ireland Limited (formerly CWS-Boco Ireland Limited)*.

From a practical point of view, it is important for the independent expert in their report (see Chapter 4) to identify any potential requirement for the company, through the examiner, to apply to court for a repudiation of an onerous lease and which properties will be affected by same. The company must also set out the reason for the repudiation of a lease to ensure that any application for its repudiation is *bona fide* for commercial purposes. It is important that meetings between the examiner, the company and its landlords are conducted as soon as the examiner is appointed to discuss the details of leases, losses to the landlords and the impact this will have on all the parties involved. All relevant and legal aspects of the repudiation will have to be considered prior to the application to the court being made. (The examiner's role in respect of repudiation is discussed in Chapter 7.)

Revenue Opposition

Revenue is in the unusual position of being an involuntary creditor of most companies that apply for the protection of the court under examinership, given that taxes are collected and paid directly by companies to Revenue in respect of the main tax headings, i.e. PAYE/PRSI, VAT and corporation tax. Accordingly, Revenue appears at most, if not all, examinership hearings.

Revenue adopts a guarded approach to schemes of arrangement, scrutinising them closely to establish if Revenue will be unfairly prejudiced. Revenue also focuses strongly on the reasonable prospect of future survival of the company as it will most likely be a creditor of the company going forward, often reluctantly.

Revenue typically votes against any scheme that does not provide for 100% of its super preferential employee PRSI claim and will also seek to maximise its preferential dividend in each case.

In the 2016 examinership of *CS Distributors Limited*, a family-owned wholesale distribution company supplying non-food convenience products to the supermarket multiples in the Republic of Ireland, Revenue objected to the proposals formulated by the examiner arising out of a failure by the company to disclose all liabilities to Revenue at the petition stage, as well as the incorrect treatment of payments to merchandisers.

Shareholder Opposition

In 2009, an examiner was appointed over *Eylewood Limited & Woodman Inns Limited*, which operated four outlets in the licensed trade and nightclub sectors. The examiner presented two schemes of arrangement to the High Court for approval. These were objected to by the company's shareholders, primarily due to the examiner's decision to treat one of the interested investors as the preferred bidder ahead of them. After considering arguments from both sides, the High Court refused to confirm the proposals. In her judgment, Ms Justice Finlay Geoghegan formed the view that the proposals did not adequately protect the companies from a contingent claim by the shareholders if they were required in the future to pay out company liabilities from personal guarantees that they had provided. Since this case and judgment, all examinerships have extinguished contingent future claims against the company from those who have guaranteed the company's debts, such claims typically being triggered when the guarantor is called upon to pay the creditor in question.

Unsecured Creditor Opposition

Though quite often a secured creditor, a bank or Revenue will be the largest single creditor, unsecured creditors may be the biggest class of creditors in terms of number. However, unsecured creditors tend to have the lowest priority and are often left with the lowest level of dividend in an examinership process. It should be noted, however, that this class of creditor must receive a higher dividend in an examinership than in a liquidation scenario.

The Appeal Process

If the examiner's proposals have been rejected by the court, it is possible for a company to appeal the decision, and this has occurred intermittently over the years. In the *Com-Plas Packaging/Scriptdale Trading* case (as discussed above) and in the *McInerney Homes* case (also referenced above), which lasted a record 331 days under the protection of the court, the Supreme Court upheld the High Court's refusal to confirm the examiner's proposals on the basis that it was unfairly prejudicial to the bank syndicate as it would have required the secured creditor to accept imposed values and forgo the opportunity of recovering a higher return under a receivership process.

A very important practical issue arises with an appeal of the examiner's scheme. A company in examinership is already trading under very challenging conditions with access to credit curtailed, reputation issues with key customers, and uncertainty and instability among key staff members. The longer the process continues, the more difficult it will be for the company to survive these challenges. Aware of this, a well-funded, obdurate creditor may choose to appeal knowing that the war of attrition that an appeal involves may assist them in collapsing the examiner's scheme. Practitioners refer to the risk of 'examinership fatigue' setting in with a company that is under court protection for an extended period of time. This phenomenon highlights two critical issues: first, the importance of the examiner acting expeditiously in carrying out their duties; and, secondly, the importance of the examiner settling contentious issues well before the confirmation hearing, wherever possible.

Implementation of a Scheme of Arrangement

In this section we will set out the legislative and practical steps required to implement a scheme of arrangement following its approval by the court.

In accordance with the legislation, "a compromise or scheme of arrangement … shall come into effect on a date fixed by the Court, which date (unless the Court deems it appropriate to fix a later one) shall be a date falling no later than 21 days after the date of the proposal's confirmation". The date fixed by the court for which the proposals come into effect is known as the 'effective date'. In normal circumstances, the effective date is set for later the same day or within 24 hours of the scheme of arrangement being approved, if there is no conditionality to the examiner's proposals, as discussed earlier in this chapter.

In situations where there are certain conditions that must be met or ful-filled before the examiner's proposals can be implemented, the effective date can be a number of weeks following approval by the court. In the 2016 examinership of *Business Mobile Security Services Limited*, a cash-in-transit and multi-disciplinary security services firm employing 250 people, the results of the meetings of members and creditors, together with the examiner's report, were presented to the court on 28 February 2017. At the confirmation hearing held on 10 March, the effective date was set for 13 April 2017. This was as a result of a new funding provider coming on board as part of the examiner's proposals. The new funding provider required a number of weeks in order to transition the compa-ny's debtor ledger from its existing invoice finance provider to its own platform. In addition, there were a number of legal documents, such as the satisfaction of the debenture by the existing finance provider and the drafting and execution of the relevant documentation by the com-pany in order to implement the new funding facilities. These all needed to be fully considered and completed prior to the effective date.

In the 2018 examinership of *Denis Moriarty The Kerries Limited*, the examiner's proposals were approved on 3 May 2018 with the effective date set for 14 June 2018. This was allowed so that the company could receive a settlement from a legal claim with one of its clients. The funds from the settlement agreement were being utilised to part-fund the examiner's proposals and pay dividends to the company's creditors.

Following confirmation of the effective date, the examiner will issue cor-respondence to all members and creditors of the company confirming:
1. the date on which the examiner's scheme of arrangement was pre-sented to the court;
2. the date on which the scheme was approved by the court;
3. the effective date and time on which the proposals are due to come into effect, at which time the examiner will also be discharged and the company ceases to be under the protection of the court.

In this correspondence, the examiner also confirms that payments under the scheme of arrangement will fall due for payment in accordance with the scheme. Dividends under the scheme are usually paid to creditors within 30 days of the effective date. This is to allow the company time to receive the balance of the funds held in escrow from the examiner's solicitor and receive any VAT refund due in respect of the examiner-ship costs incurred, as set out in the escrow agreement (see Chapter 8).

However, in the case of secured creditors, where their claim is not being restructured and they are being paid a dividend in respect of the value of their security, the secured creditor should receive their dividend within five days. This happens in order to allow the examiner sufficient time to deliver the required documents to the Companies Registration Office (CRO) as required by the Companies Act 2014.

In order for the company to discharge all dividends as required under the scheme, the investment funds, as per the investment agreement, less the costs and remuneration of the examiner, are typically returned to the company. It is the company's responsibility to make the dividend payments to all creditors, as the examiner will be discharged by the effective date; however, the examiner can assist in making the dividends if requested to do so by the company.

The examiner (or former examiner at this stage) is also required to submit a copy of the final court order and scheme of arrangement approved by the court, including any modifications, to the CRO (or the Department of the Registrar of Companies in Cyprus). The examiner is also required to provide a copy of the examiner's report to the Office of the Director of Corporate Enforcement.

KEY POINTS: THE SCHEME OF ARRANGEMENT

1. The scheme of arrangement is formulated once the investment process has been completed and sets out how the company will emerge from examinership, detailing the dividends payable to all classes of creditors.
2. After the examiner has issued the scheme of arrangement, meetings are convened with members and creditors to allow them to vote on the scheme.
3. Notices of meetings should be sent no less than three days before the date of the meeting.
4. For a scheme to be approved by a class of member or creditor, the majority of that class must vote in favour of the scheme in number and value. The scheme must be accepted by at least one class of compromised creditor in order to allow the examiner to return to court and seek confirmation. There is no minimum requirement for shareholder acceptance; members cannot veto a scheme of arrangement.

5. At least three creditors of the company that are entitled to vote must be represented at the meetings for the meeting to be quorate.
6. Once the court has considered the examiner's report on the outcome of the meetings, it can confirm the proposed scheme of arrangement, refuse the proposals or approve the proposals, subject to whatever modifications it considers necessary.
7. If the scheme of arrangement is rejected, court protection ceases and a receiver can be appointed to the company by its secured creditors, or a liquidator may be appointed by the court or by a meeting of creditors.
8. A creditor or member may oppose the scheme of arrangement if they are treated unfairly in comparison with other creditors or members in the same class, or in comparison to how they would have been treated in a liquidation or receivership.
9. If the examiner's proposals are rejected, the company or a creditor can appeal the decision.
10. The legislation sets out that the scheme of arrangement shall come into effect no later than 21 days following the date of its confirmation.

10.

The Costs of Examinership

- Introduction
- Costs of a Successful Examinership
- Costs of an Unsuccessful Examinership
- Key Points: The Costs of Examinership

Introduction

The costs of examinership have been a cause for much debate over the years, with a perception that examinership is a mechanism suitable only for larger companies and that it is too expensive a process for small and medium-sized enterprise (SMEs) to engage in. This perception started to change with the introduction of 'examinership-lite' to the legislation by the Companies (Miscellaneous Provisions) Act 2013, which was mentioned in Chapter 2. The most significant change this Act made to existing company law was in respect of the role of the Circuit Court in overseeing the examinership process, with the intention that the process would become more affordable and thus more attractive to SMEs. While there was a mechanism to apply to the Circuit Court for examinership under previous legislation, this provision was rarely utilised. In practical terms, until the introduction of the 2013 legislation, the High Court was the only court that heard examinership applications.

The costs of an examinership can be split into two stages, the petition stage and the examinership stage.

The Petition Stage

When a company takes the decision to seek court protection under examinership there are certain initial costs the petitioner must bear in order to make an application. The costs incurred in respect of this process will relate to the initial *ex-parte* (one side only) application and the full hearing of the petition to appoint an examiner. These costs can run to circa €15,000 plus VAT and outlay, and typically include the following:
- the independent expert – preparation of the independent expert's report (IER);
- a solicitor – preparation and filing of the petition with the court in addition to court attendance;
- a barrister – reviewing the petition prior to its presentation to the court, as well as acting as the petitioner's advocate in court.

The Examinership Stage

Following the granting of court protection, the costs associated with an examinership are dependent on a wide range of variables, which most notably include the length of time a company remains under court protection, the complexity of each case and whether an examiner has been appointed over a single entity or a group structure. There may also be a requirement for the examiner to engage certain third-party professionals during the process. For example, where a situation arises that a company asset is subject to a charge from a secured creditor there will be a requirement to obtain a professional valuation. Any such out-lay incurred by an examiner will impact on the cost of the process. The rates charged by an examiner tend to be in line with those approved by Mr Justice Kelly in *Missford Limited t/a Residence Members Club* (*'Missford'*) in 2010 (discussed further below).

There are a number of steps involved in agreeing and discharging the costs of an examinership and these steps vary, depending on whether the examinership has been successful or unsuccessful.

Costs of a Successful Examinership

In a successful examinership, the professional costs incurred by an examiner and their advisors are discharged from the investment sum that forms part of the investment agreement (see Chapter 8). Prior to executing an investment agreement, the investor will be made aware of the costs associated with the process, usually in the form of a schedule of costs.

Approval of Examinership Costs

As discussed in Chapter 9, following the convening of the various meetings of the members and creditors, if they have obtained the required support for their proposed scheme of arrangement, the examiner will return to court to submit the final examiner's report and seek approval of the scheme they have formulated. Usually included in this report will be a summary of professional fees incurred. Legal counsel for the examiner will take the court through the report and will highlight details of the investment and direct the court to the summary of professional costs. As it is the court that ulti-mately approves the scheme, including the professional costs of the examinership, and creditors are entitled to transparency regarding the costs associated with the process, it is important for the examiner and their advisors to maintain a complete and accurate schedule of costs incurred.

Discharging of Examinership Costs

The discharging of examinership costs can only occur after the approval of those costs by the court. Such approval is normally obtained at the same time as the scheme is confirmed. However, it is also possible for the examiner to seek an interim payment of costs on account. In the 2017 case *JP McKenna & Sons Limited* an order was made for an interim payment of examinership costs from the company's own resources during the protection period and in advance of the scheme stage.

It is important to note that the company is entitled to reclaim VAT on all professional fees paid, which can be substantial, depending on the quantum of costs incurred, and can provide a company with a significant uplift in its cash flow. The examiner and their professional advisors are required to submit invoices to the company upon receipt of the payment of their professional costs.

Costs of an Unsuccessful Examinership

Application for Costs

Where an examinership has not resulted in the turnaround of a company's fortunes, the former examiner is required to make an application for payment of the examiner's remuneration (under section 554 of the Companies Act), expenses and legal fees to the court which heard the petition for examinership and subsequently oversaw the process. If the company has gone into liquidation or receivership, creditors' claims will be adversely affected, as explained in the "Statement of Affairs" section in Chapter 5. In addition, Revenue usually request to be a notice party to any application made by the former examiner in respect of their costs.

The application is made *ex parte* and directions as to service (i.e. how the application will be served) and the date of hearing of the application will be provided by the court. The application is grounded on an affidavit from the (former) examiner and generally includes the following:
• details of the work carried out during the period of the examinership;
• a summary of time spent on the examinership by each member of the examiner's staff, their position within the firm, the hourly rate for each individual staff member (it is important that staff are assigned to deal with matters at the appropriate level of experience and knowledge, and that their charge-out rates reflect these);
• details of legal work carried out and a summary of the related legal costs, including counsel and outlay expenses, specifying hourly rates charged;

- a summary of the amount of related expenses incurred during the examinership;
- details of the utilisation of company resources, including staff and facilities (did the examiner manage the examinership effectively by using the resources and facilities of the company wherever possible?);
- details of any liabilities certified by the examiner (as discussed in Chapter 7).

Some of the notice parties (including Revenue and/or the largest creditor) to the application for costs may have queries or have indicated that they will object at the hearing of the application. The matter may not be straightforward and could result in a lengthy hearing that requires affidavits to be exchanged between the parties. In order to minimise costs and reduce the time required to deal with any objection, it is preferable and to the benefit of all parties involved to deal with any queries, iron out any issues raised and, where necessary, reach an agreement in respect of the examinership costs with the notice parties prior to returning to court. This is to the benefit of all parties involved.

The sum that the court awards to the former examiner will take account of the following factors:
- any prior agreement with the company and/or investor in an investment agreement entered into (see Chapter 8);
- complexity of the issues arising in the case;
- opposition to the level of costs sought.

Priority of the Costs

With the exception of certified liabilities deemed vital for the survival of the company, the former examiner's costs, once sanctioned by the court, are prioritised above the claims of **all** other creditors, including:
- preferential creditors;
- fixed-charge creditors;
- a receiver's costs;
- a liquidator's costs; and
- the company's trading costs.

The intention behind the priority afforded to the examiner's costs is that companies may not be in a position to avail of the examinership process unless they can guarantee to the professionals involved that they can be paid from the assets of the company. If such priority did not exist, many companies that have successfully emerged from the process may not have been considered, in the first instance, by insolvency practitioners as being suitable candidates as there would be no means to discharge costs in the event of a failed examinership. This is particularly relevant where a company is not asset-rich but may require examinership to protect intangible assets such as its brand, intellectual property, goodwill or other tangible assets, for example in the form of leasehold interests.

It is often required that the court determines the costs of a failed examinership. The law on the matter is largely derived from the principles outlined in the *Sharmane Limited* case, the 2009 examinership of the Thomas Read Group (13 related companies operating some of Dublin's best known bars and restaurants), where ultimately, ACC Bank and Ulster Bank Ireland succeeded in opposing the examinership where an examiner was appointed. Following the unsuccessful conclusion of the examinership, an application was made to the court by the former examiner for remuneration, expenses and legal fees in the normal manner.

In the *Sharmane Limited* case, a dispute arose between the former examiner and the appointed receiver in relation to the timing and priority of the examiner's payments. The former examiner argued that he was entitled to have his fees discharged out of the company's revenue (income). The receiver, however, argued that this payment should not be prioritised before the sale of the company's assets. The court directed payment to the former examiner out of the revenue of the business, i.e. literally from the takings in the tills, in priority to all other outgoings and costs in the receivership.

As mentioned in Chapter 7, supplier accounts certified by the examiner in respect of expenses will not have priority over any claims by creditors secured by mortgage, charge or lien, or other debts of a fixed nature. They do, however, have priority over the claims of floating-charge creditors.

The Quantum

The court has jurisdiction to consider the work carried out by the examiner, the quantum of that work and the expenses incurred during the process to ensure that they are deemed appropriate on a case-by-case basis.

In considering the work carried out by the examiner and their staff, the court will ask a number of questions:
1. Was the work carried out within the statutory requirements of the Companies Act 2014?
2. Were there unusual circumstances in the case that warranted the examiner to spend more time or not use the resources of the company

(e.g. where the books and records of the company were inadequately maintained to allow the examiner to carry out their duty)?
3. If there are a number of companies in a group and all are in examinership, have the timesheets of the examiner and their staff reflected time spent on each case appropriately?
4. Did the examiner hold executive functions and was therefore required to spend more time in actually running the company?

Chargeable Rates   As part of the application process, the charge-out rates sought by the former examiner and their staff will be also be given due consideration by the court. In the 2010 examinership case of *Missford Limited*, which operated "Residence", a private-members club in Dublin, Mr Justice Kelly heard an application for the remuneration costs and expenses of an interim examiner. Mr Justice Kelly highlighted that the court must not only assess the hourly rates of the examiner and their staff, but also the reasonableness of their renumeration. In this case, the former interim examiner explained to the court how the hourly rate was calculated. As discussed in Chapter 7, the role the examiner plays will depend on whether or not they are required to take on executive functions and the extent and scale of the business operated by the company/group of companies under examinership. This case highlighted the importance of examiners applying to the court if they feel that it is necessary that they take on executive powers, as this would not usually be required in the normal course. A formal application to the court to assume such executive powers will serve to support the examiner spending time on work that goes beyond the level of that envisaged by the legislation.

In this case, the court reduced the examiner's hourly rate (a partner in the professional firm) to €375 and made a blanket reduction of 16% in the total rates sought.

To date, the reduced hourly rate for examiners as set in the *Missford Limited* case remains the default position for applications for fees in unsuccessful examinerships. Interestingly, the charge-out rates set in *Missford Limited* have also been adopted for remuneration in liquidation and administration cases.

Similar provisions apply to legal fees incurred by the examiner. In dealing with the examiner's application, it may be that the court decides that the amount provided for by the legal counsel must be assessed and determined by the Taxing Master (see below). Each case will be determined individually, depending primarily on the reasonableness and the level of any opposition to the quantum of costs being sought.

The *Missford Limited* case is also the primary reference for the court in assessing the reasonableness of the legal fees sought and how it considers whether the legal work carried out was within the remit of the legislation. In this case, the court referred the matter to the Taxing Master with specific instructions. The Taxing Master provides an independent and impartial assessment of legal costs incurred by an individual or company involved in litigation. In this regard, Mr Justice Kelly stated:

> "Insofar as the legal costs claimed are concerned, I propose to refer them to the Taxing Master. In taxing the bill, the Taxing Master ought to bear in mind the observations that I have made concerning charge out rates in respect of professional fees. He should also bear in mind that the only legal fees which are allowable are those which impact directly upon the work properly undertaken by the interim examiner by reference to his limited role. Legal fees cannot be recovered for work undertaken outside the scope ... of [the examiner's] powers."

Other Costs

While legal fees and expenses are a feature of all examinership cases, the process does not necessarily have to be costly in this regard. Direct correspondence between the parties rather than through legal advisors is generally a more efficient form of communication and allows matters to be agreed, if possible, on a more straightforward basis. This sets parameters for all parties involved and helps to avoid the duplication of work.

In the event that Revenue is listed as a notice party, it will request that its costs are paid for its court appearances. Similarly, if legal fees and expenses are referred to the Taxing Master, this will also give rise to further costs.

KEY POINTS: THE COSTS OF EXAMINERSHIP

1. When a company initially petitions the court, it incurs costs for an independent expert to prepare their report, a solicitor to prepare the petition and a barrister to review the petition and advocate in court.

171

2. In a successful examinership, the professional costs incurred by an examiner and their advisors are borne from the investment sum that forms part of the investment agreement. Rates charged are in line with those approved by Mr Justice Kelly in *Missford Limited t/a Residence Members Club* in 2010.

3. Where the examinership has been unsuccessful, the former examiner is required to make an application for payment of remuneration, expenses and legal fees to the court that oversaw the process.

4. The court has jurisdiction to consider the work carried out by the examiner and the expenses incurred during the process to ensure that they are deemed appropriate; they will be considered on a case-by-case basis.

11.

The Future of Examinership

- Introduction
- EU Directive on Restructuring
- Effectiveness of 'Examinership Lite'
- Conclusion
- Afterword: The Summary Rescue Process

Introduction

Table 11.1 below tracks the number of jobs saved by examinership in both SMEs and large businesses in Ireland since 2010 and clearly shows the impact the process has had in protecting employment. In total, in the 10 years from 2010 to 2020 inclusive, 16,475 jobs were saved in businesses that successfully came through the process.

TABLE 11.1: JOBS SAVED UNDER EXAMINERSHIP SINCE 2010

Number of Jobs Saved	
2010	419
2011	574
2012	5965
2013	2242
2014	1243
2015	1251
2016	2132
2017	957
2018	501
2019	598
2020	593
TOTAL	**16,475**

(Source: Baker Tilly SME Examinership Index)

It is clear from this annual index that despite the very low number of companies that petitioned for examinership in these years, the process played a significant role in protecting employment and reducing the cost of redundancies to the Exchequer as the country recovered slowly from the financial crisis of 2008–2009 and the subsequent economic collapse.

EU Directive on Restructuring

It appears that the European Union is determined that the key principles of examinership become the norm across Europe and since 2019 they have been reflected in EU law. The introduction of examinership in Cyprus by the 'troika' of the European Commission, European Central Bank (ECB) and the International Monetary Fund (IMF) in 2015 was the first practical manifestation of high-level initiatives that have been ongoing for many years. Research from the European Commission has highlighted that every year in the EU circa 200,000 companies become insolvent, which results in circa 1.7 million job losses.[1] At the time of writing, half of all Europeans say they will not start a business due to the fear of the consequences of failure. The effects of the banking crises in Europe from 2008 to 2013 still reverberate with the various EU authorities, which are determined to have structures in place that increase economic stability. In November 2016, the European Commission announced a proposed new Directive that would align all EU Member States in terms of the availability of business restructuring processes that are akin to examinership. This EU Directive aimed at harmonising Member State restructuring and insolvency laws (the 'Directive') entered into force on 16 July 2019. Member States are required to adopt and publish compliant laws and regulations by 17 July 2021.[2]

The stated objective of this new EU Directive is to contribute to the proper functioning of the internal market and remove obstacles to the exercise of fundamental EU freedoms, such as the free movement of capital and freedom of establishment, which result from differences between national laws and procedures on preventive restructuring, insolvency and second chance. Harmonising insolvency procedures will decrease risks in restructuring by allowing for the proper functioning of the internal market and removing obstacles to the exercise of fundamental freedoms. This will, in turn, increase the likelihood of new investment in companies seeking capital to restructure and refinance.

The Directive also places employees centre stage in any restructuring of a trading business. Without affecting workers' fundamental rights and freedoms, the Directive aims to ensure that:
• viable enterprises and entrepreneurs in financial difficulties, including individual entrepreneurs who are economically viable, have access to effective national preventive restructuring frameworks which enable them to continue operating;
• honest, over-indebted entrepreneurs have a second chance once debts have been cleared following a formal insolvency process; and

---

[1] "Insolvency: Commission recommends new approach to rescue businesses and give honest entrepreneurs a second chance". European Commission, Press Release, 12 March 2014.

[2] Directive (EU) 2019/1023 of the European Parliament and of the Council of 20 June 2019 on preventive restructuring frameworks, on discharge of debt and disqualifications, and on measures to increase the efficiency of procedures concerning restructuring, insolvency and discharge of debt.

- the effectiveness of restructuring, insolvency and discharge procedures is improved, particularly with a view to shortening their length to no more than four months.

Targeted measures for EU Member States will be introduced to increase the efficiency of insolvency, restructuring and discharge procedures. This will reduce the excessive length and costs of procedures in many Member States, which result in legal uncertainty for creditors and investors, and low recovery rates of unpaid debts. The new rules will observe the following key principles to ensure insolvency and restructuring frameworks are consistent and efficient throughout the EU:
- Companies in financial difficulties, especially SMEs, will have access to early warning tools to help them detect a deteriorating business situation and ensure restructuring at an early stage.
- Flexible preventive restructuring frameworks will simplify lengthy, complex and costly court proceedings. Where necessary, national courts will be involved to safeguard the interests of stakeholders.
- Debtors will benefit from a time-limited 'breathing space' from creditors' claims for a maximum of four months in order to facilitate negotiations and successful restructuring.
- Dissenting minority creditors and shareholders will not be able to block restructuring plans, though their legitimate interests will be safeguarded.
- New financing will be specifically protected, increasing the chances of successful restructuring.
- Throughout the preventive restructuring procedures, workers will enjoy full labour law protection in accordance with EU law.
- Training, specialisation of practitioners and courts, and the use of technology (e.g. online filing of claims, notifications to creditors, etc.) will improve the efficiency and length of insolvency, restructuring and second-chance procedures.

The Directive identifies that restructuring should enable enterprises and personally liable entrepreneurs in financial difficulties to continue in business in whole or in part, by changing the composition, conditions or structure of their assets and liabilities, or of their capital structure, including by the sale of assets or parts of the business or the business itself.

Preventive restructuring frameworks should, above all, enable enterprises to restructure rapidly at an early stage and avoid the insolvency and liquidation of viable companies. Such rapid preventive frameworks, based on the debtor-in-possession model, where the management of the insolvent company retains executive powers, should prevent job losses and the loss of knowledge and skills, and maximise the total value to creditors in comparison to what they would have received in the event of the liquidation of the company's assets, as well as to owners and the economy as a whole. They should also prevent the build-up of non-performing loans. In the restructuring process, the rights of all parties involved should be protected, including those of workers. At the same time, non-viable businesses with no prospect of survival should be liquidated as quickly as possible. The availability of preventive rapid restructuring procedures would ensure that action is taken before companies default on their loans, thereby helping to reduce the risk of loans becoming non-performing in cyclical downturns and cushioning the adverse impact on the financial sector. A significant percentage of businesses and jobs could be saved if preventive procedures existed in all Member States where businesses' places of establishment, assets or creditors are situated.

All of the concepts of the EU Directive sit squarely within the fundamental concepts of the examinership process that has existed in Ireland since 1990 and Cyprus since 2015. Though the prescience of Irish legislators appears to have gone unrecognised by the EU, it is likely that the legal concepts they introduced will become standard in the EU 30 years after being introduced in Ireland.

Effectiveness of 'Examinership-Lite'

As discussed in Chapter 1 and again in Chapter 10, the Companies (Miscellaneous Provisions) Act 2013 introduced 'examinership-lite' with the intention of making examinership more accessible to struggling SMEs. In the words of then Minister for Jobs, Enterprise and Innovation, Richard Bruton:

> "This will mean that more businesses can survive their current difficulties and start to grow, meaning crucially that more jobs will be saved and more jobs will be created in this hugely important part of the economy."

One of the main innovations of Circuit Court examinership is that companies can petition for examinership to the Circuit Court; before its introduction, all petitions for examinership were heard, and all examinerships overseen, by the High Court. This was intended to make the process less costly and therefore more accessible.

At the time of its introduction, it was predicted that the legal fees associated with examinership would be circa 30% lower for the Circuit

Court option. While legal costs have certainly dropped since the move to the Circuit Court, the low number of petitioning companies in the period from 2012 to 2018 indicate that the option of the Circuit Court has not had the desired effect of saving a greater number of businesses.

Other difficulties with the Circuit Court option are more practical. Moving the process to regional locations ignored the reality that the vast majority of insolvency practitioners (lawyers and accountants) are based in Dublin. Therefore, the effort to reduce costs has not been as effective as was hoped, as the move to the Circuit Court has increased very significantly the time required to travel to regional locations by teams for sometimes very routine applications, for example to extend the period of the examinership.

However, the main difficulty relates to the timing of court sittings. Examinership applications are made with extreme urgency, where generally a company is about to close down if it is not protected by court order. Therefore, examinerships tend not to wait for the appropriate court to be sitting in a convenient location. This issue is accentuated during the summer court vacation when many petitioning companies have no option but to petition the High Court in Dublin due to the lack of an available Circuit Court sitting to facilitate the examinership.

While it is clear that there were certainly good intentions behind the move to the Circuit Court, it is difficult to argue that the introduction of the Circuit Court option has been an untrammelled success.

Conclusion

All of those who have contributed to this book have been fortunate to see and experience the benefits of successful examinerships on many occasions.

An examinership can often end with an employee meeting, at which point, people who have lived during the restructuring phase with uncertainty about losing their jobs are informed that their employer has been rescued and their livelihoods are therefore secure. Such meetings effectively illustrate and reinforce the overarching purpose of examinership: to save viable jobs in viable enterprises.

Examinership is **not**:
• for saving the investment of a shareholder where that venture has proven unsuccessful; or
• a process for whitewashing the illegal actions of directors; or

- a recovery process for creditors, secured or otherwise (although it must give creditors a better return than they can expect in a winding up – see Chapter 9).

Examinership is essentially about finding a better practical outcome for all stakeholders from a crisis insolvency event. A going concern outcome inevitably preserves value and lessens the damage caused by business failure. Stakeholders may not be happy with an examiner's proposals, but a good scheme of arrangement is where the rights of creditors are struck with such a fine balance that creditors who may be unhappy with the scheme decide to accept it, as the outcome for them may be worse if the business closed its doors. On very rare occasions, examinership cases can result in creditors being paid in full.

The vast majority of companies that enter examinership emerge from the process successfully. Many thousands of jobs have been saved and the Irish State has been protected from enormous redundancy and social welfare costs that would have been triggered by the failure of those companies that were saved. Both Cyprus, and more recently the EU generally, have copied the core principles of the process and therefore it appears that it is very much here to stay.

It is for all these reasons that examinership is generally viewed as a positive rescue tool by the vast majority of business people and practitioners.

Afterword: The Summary Rescue Process

The economic fallout from the Covid-19 crisis of 2020–2021 accelerated calls in Ireland for a new streamlined process for the rescue of small companies. This became a focus of the work of the Company Law Review Group (CLRG) during 2020. The CLRG is a statutory advisory body charged with advising the Minister for Business, Enterprise and Innovation (the Minister) on the review and development of Irish company law. It was accorded statutory advisory status by the Company Law Enforcement Act 2001, which was continued under section 958 of the Companies Act 2014.

The CLRG operates on the basis of a two-year work programme which is determined by the Minister, in consultation with the CLRG. The CLRG consists of members who have expertise and an interest in the development of company law, including practitioners (the legal profession and accountants), users (business and trade unions), regulators (implementation and enforcement bodies) and representatives from government departments, including the Department of Enterprise, Trade and Employment and the Revenue Commissioners. The CLRG was established to "monitor, review and advise the Minister on matters concerning company law". In so doing, it is required to "seek to promote enterprise, facilitate commerce, simplify the operation of the Act, enhance corporate governance and encourage commercial probity" (section 959 of the Companies Act 2014).

During its 2020 review, the CLRG recognised the success of the examinership process and recommended to the Minister that it be maintained in its current form. However, it also critically recommended the introduction of a new simpler process for SME businesses. The process should be distinct from examinership and have a separate name, which the CLRG recommends be the 'Summary Rescue Process'.

The procedure should be available to 'small companies' as defined in the Companies Act, meaning companies that satisfy two of these three criteria:
- annual turnover of up to €12 million;
- a balance sheet total of up to €6 million;
- up to 50 employees.

The CLRG further recommends that the Summary Rescue Process have the following features:
- The process would commence by a resolution of the company's directors rather than by an application to court as in examinership.
- Instead of running for 70 to 100 days (or longer under the Companies (Miscellaneous Provisions) (Covid-19) Act 2020, which enables up to 150 days) as in examinership, the process would aim to conclude within a shorter period.
- The company's directors would commence the process following advice from a qualified insolvency practitioner as to the company's viability, subject to a compromise with creditors and/or introduction of new capital.
- The insolvency practitioner would oversee the process and assist the company's directors in preparing a rescue plan for approval by creditors.
- A vote of the creditors to support a rescue plan should be required, by a 50% +1 majority in value, as in examinership, rather than the 75% vote required in a scheme of arrangement under Part 9 of the Companies Act.
- Cross-class cram-down of debts would be available as part of the process, with court approval of any cross-class cram-down required in the formats proposed, designed with a view to reducing costs.

- The possibility of approval of a rescue plan without an application to court should be examined, provided there is no objection from any creditor involved.

Generally, the Minister tends to accept and implement CLRG recommendations. Therefore, it appears likely that the Summary Rescue Process will soon join examinership as an effective restructuring tool for Irish businesses as they grapple with the economic effects of the Covid-19 pandemic.

Appendix A.
Case Studies

In this appendix we have included some case studies of companies that have successfully navigated the examinership process.

- **Multi-unit Pharmacy Operator**
- **Multi-unit Fashion Retailer**
- **Mechanical Engineering Contractor**
- **Hotel**
- **Construction Company**

Multi-unit Pharmacy Operator

This pharmacy chain operated from seven shopping centre units and traded profitably for many years before becoming loss-making following the onset of recession.

The critical issue faced by the company was being tied into long-term, upwards-only onerous leases, at far above market terms. All other variable costs of the business were successfully reduced in line with turnover by the directors, but the company was unable to reduce its main overhead: rent.

The company entered examinership and the weakest trading store was immediately closed. Negotiations took place with other landlords using the examinership framework and reductions of between 50%–80% were achieved. The reductions were sufficient in themselves to turn around the company's fortunes and make it profitable.

A cash business, the company operated at a surplus during the protection period and utilised that surplus to fund a scheme of arrangement for all creditors. It emerged debt free following the 100-day process with six stores still trading and 25 jobs intact.

Multi-unit Fashion Retailer

This group of companies involved two trading entities and one holding company, which was the shareholder for the two trading companies. The trading companies operated seven retail units across Ireland. The companies entered examinership in the summer of 2013. The critical issues facing the trading companies at the time were reduction in turnover as a result of falling disposal income in the wider economy and unsustainable rent levels for their trading stores. The independent expert was clear in his report that a condition of the companies' survival was the renegotiation or repudiation of leases entered into by the companies.

Immediately following his appointment, the examiner contacted each of the companies' landlords in order to update them on developments and seek to hold initial meetings with all. At the commencement of the examinership period, the companies' total annual rent bill was in the amount of €950,000.

During the examinership process, the companies closed and handed back one lease. This unit was loss-making and even on reduced rental terms the store would remain loss-making. No repudiation application was required as the company operating the store leased the unit from another company within the wider group not forming part of the examinership process. A fixed charge receiver was appointed over the assets of this related company and the receiver accepted the handing back of the lease. Following protracted negotiations with all of the companies' landlords, the examiner achieved a reduction in annual rental payments in the amount of €296,000 in respect of the stores that were continuing to trade. This represented an annual reduction of 38% on the contractual rents. The examiner also negotiated a number of rent-free periods in order to allow the companies further breathing space when exiting the examinership process.

The examiner's scheme of arrangement was successfully approved by the creditors and the High Court in November 2013, with all companies exiting the examinership process. In total, 31 jobs were saved including those in the store that was closed during the protection period as these staff members were redeployed to other stores.

Mechanical Engineering Contractor

This group of companies consisted of two trading companies and two holding companies. The trade of the companies involved mechanical engineering and the installation of pre-insulated and ducting panels.

The companies traded profitably for a number of years until 2016 when they started to experience difficulties. As with many contracting companies, losses on specific contracts precipitated the companies' insolvency. Other issues faced by the companies were:
• cash-flow problems;
• the threat of winding up orders;
• delay in securing investment;
• loss of key management.

The key risk for the companies when entering the examinership process was the loss or cancellation of contracts as a result of seeking the protection of the court. However, the appointed examiner negotiated with the companies' clients to ensure the continued operation of all contracts the companies were engaged on, with the exception of one that was onerous and loss-making. As a result of the scaling back of this contract during the examinership, the companies were able to focus their resources on more profitable contracts to ensure their survival.

The examiner was successful in obtaining new investment and formulating a scheme of arrangement, which resulted in the saving of over 70 jobs in the west of Ireland.

Hotel

This company was involved in the operation of a hotel, night club and bar in County Wicklow. The company's business commenced in 1984 and the hotel traded profitably for a number of years. However, the following difficulties for the company became very apparent with the onset of recession:

- difficulties in the hotel industry as a whole, including oversupply of hotel rooms as a result of sector-specific tax incentives;
- management issues;
- significant contingent liabilities as a result of third-party claims against the company.

The company became insolvent and entered examinership.

During the 100-day protection period, new investment was secured for the company from the existing directors. The company reduced its costs, secured a tax clearance certificate and returned to profitability.

The company emerged from examinership after reaching agreement with its creditors to pay them a 10% dividend on their debts. The Revenue Commissioners were paid 20% in full and final settlement of arrears of tax owing.

The scheme of arrangement was approved by the High Court and the company exited the process with 45 jobs intact and all historical creditors fully discharged.

Construction Company

This company is a reputable building contractor with a history of successful large-scale building projects for over 30 years. It was engaged on six projects at the time court protection was sought, a number of which related to the provision of social housing units.

The issues faced by the company were:

- low gross profit margin in a very competitive market;
- a disputed claim on a project;
- losses on investment in development lands;
- an unsustainable level of secured debt.

The key risk for the company when entering the examinership process was the cancellation of contracts by clients as a result of the application for court protection. Work had already ceased on a number of the sites due to the uncertainty surrounding the company's future. However, the appointed examiner was successful in negotiating with the company's clients to ensure the continued operation of all viable contracts on which the company was engaged, subject to securing investment and the approval of a scheme of arrangement by the High Court. By eliminating onerous and loss-making contracts the company was better positioned to focus on existing profitable contracts while also actively seeking to secure further work.

The examiner was successful in obtaining new investment and formulating a scheme of arrangement, which was approved by the High Court, resulting in 24 jobs being saved while also agreeing a settlement in relation to the secured debt. This ensured that the company returned to work on viable ongoing projects, which is now allowing for the completion of much-needed social housing units.

Appendix B. Statement of Insolvency Practice 19B

Appointment as Examiner or Independent Expert under Part 10, Companies Act 2014 – Republic of Ireland

Updated 1 January 2018

Introduction

1. The Statement of Insolvency Practice is one of a series issued by the Institute of Chartered Accountants in Ireland to insolvency practitioners with a view to maintaining standards by setting out required practice and harmonising members' approach to particular aspects of insolvency.

2. The purpose of Statements of Insolvency Practice is to set out basic principles and essential procedures with which insolvency practitioners are required to comply. Departure from the standards set out in the Statements of Insolvency Practice is a matter that may be considered by the Institute for the purposes of possible disciplinary or regulatory action.

3. The supplemental practical guidance is intended to assist the insolvency practitioner to comply with the Statement. The insolvency practitioner is entitled to adopt alternative procedures in the detailed circumstances of a particular assignment where they judge that tailored approach to be more appropriate.

4. The nature and extent of the work involved in each assignment will differ, but, generally, will include compliance with the standards outlined below.

5. This Statement addresses:

   - the statutory basis for appointment of an examiner and an interim examiner,
   - the independent expert's report,
   - role of the examiner,
   - report of the examiner, and
   - powers and duties of directors of the company.

6. Remuneration of the examiner is dealt with in the Statement of Insolvency Practice 9B 'Remuneration of Insolvency Office Holders'.

Scope

7. The Statement addresses the insolvency practitioner's responsibility when appointed as an examiner of a company, and the responsibility of a practitioner when acting as independent expert.

Principles

8. The Statement has been prepared taking account of the following principles:

    (a) Ensure members are familiar with their legal and professional obligations when appointed examiner or an independent expert to a company.
    (b) Practitioners must maintain proper records and account for how they have discharged their obligations in accordance with the law.

Requirements

9. The statutory framework governing the examination process is set out under Part 10, Companies Act, 2014 (the 'Act').
10. Specific requirements governing the examination process are also set out in Order 74A of the Rules of the Superior Courts (Companies Act 2014) 2015, which came into operation on 1 July 2015 and for "small" companies Order 53A of the Rules of the Circuit Court Rules (Companies Act 2014) 2015, which came into operation on 9 November 2015. These rules are available at www.courts.ie.
11. Insolvency practitioners should have regard to the impact of Court decisions on developing practice.

Appointment of an Examiner

12. In order to appoint an examiner, a petition must be presented to the court. The petition will nominate a person to be appointed as examiner to a company and may be presented by any of the following, individually or collectively – the company, the directors, a creditor (a contingent or prospective creditor including an employee), or a member(s) with a shareholding of more than 10%, of the company.
13. The petition must be accompanied by:

    (i)   a consent signed by the person nominated to be examiner;
    (ii) a report in relation to the company by an independent expert; and
    (iii) a copy of a compromise or scheme of arrangement in relation to the company's affairs if one has been prepared for approval by interested parties.

14. The court may then appoint an examiner to the company, where it appears to the court that:

    (i) the company is, or is likely to be, unable to pay its debts (on either a balance sheet or cashflow test);
    (ii) there is no resolution for the winding-up of the company; and
    (iii)no order has been made for the winding-up of the company.

15. The court will only make an order if it is satisfied that there is a 'reasonable prospect of survival of the company and the whole or any part of its undertaking as a going concern'.

16. In the case, *Re: Tuskar Resouces plc*, Judge McCracken stated:

    "If the Court is "satisfied", it must be satisfied on the evidence before it, which is in the first instance the evidence of the petitioner. If that evidence does not satisfy the Court, the order cannot be made, and in my view that is tantamount to saying there is an onus of proof on the petitioner at the initial stage to satisfy the Court that there is a reasonable prospect of survival.".

17. In the case of *Vantive Holdings and Others*, Judge Murray stated:

    "In order to be satisfied that a company has a reasonable prospect of survival as a going concern the Court must have before it sufficient evidence or material which will permit it to arrive at such a conclusion on the basis of an objective appraisal of that evidence or material.....

    The opinion of the independent accountant as set out in the report which a petitioner is required to provide to the Court under the provisions of the Act must be given due weight. Again, the weight to be attached to the accountant's opinion will depend on the degree and extent to which he supports that opinion by his or her own objective reasoning and the appraisal of material or factors relied upon for reaching his or her conclusions."

18. The court will not make an order under certain circumstances, including, where a company has obligations in relation to a bank asset that has been transferred to NAMA unless the company has submitted a copy of the petition to NAMA and the court has heard from NAMA in making the order.

19. The court will not hear a petition for appointment of an examiner if a receiver has been appointed to the company for a continuous period of at least three days prior to the date of the presentation of the petition. If the petitioner is a contingent or prospective creditor

the court will not hear the petition unless the petitioner has provided reasonable security for costs.

20. The court may decline to hear or continue hearing a petition if it appears to the court that the petitioner or independent expert failed to disclose material information or exercise utmost good faith in the preparation and presentation of the petition or independent expert's report respectively.

21. The effect of presenting a petition to appoint an examiner, is to place company under court protection for a period of 70 days (unless the petition is earlier withdrawn or refused by the court) commencing from the date the petition was presented. During this period, the company is protected from a number of actions, including but not limited to, for example, proceedings to wind up the company, appointment of a receiver, crystallisation of security charges, repossession orders.

22. Under certain circumstances, the court may grant an extension not exceeding 30 days on application by the examiner.

Independent Expert's Report

Independent Expert

23. As noted in paragraph 13, the petition should be accompanied by an independent expert's report. This report should be prepared by a person who is either the statutory auditor of the company or who is qualified to be appointed as an examiner of the company.

Independent Expert's Report – Legislative Requirements

24. The independent expert's report should consist of the following:
    (i)   the names and addresses of the officers of the company;
    (ii)   the names of any other bodies corporate of which the directors of the company are also directors;
    (iii) a statement of affairs of the company;
    (iv)   their opinion as to, whether:
    - any deficiency between the assets and liabilities of the company has been satisfactorily accounted for;
    - the company, and the whole or any part of its undertaking, would have a reasonable prospect of survival as a going concern and a statement of the conditions which he/she considers are essential to ensure such survival;

- the formulation, acceptance and confirmation of proposals for a compromise or scheme of arrangement would offer a reasonable prospect of the survival of the company, and the whole or any part of its undertaking, as a going concern;
- an attempt to continue the whole or any part of the undertaking would be likely to be more advantageous to the members as a whole and the creditors as a whole than a winding-up of the company;
- the facts disclosed would warrant further inquiries;
- the work of the examiner would be assisted by a direction of the court.

(v) recommendations as to the course they think should be taken in relation to the company, including, draft proposals for a compromise or scheme of arrangement;

(vi) recommendations as to which liabilities incurred before the presentation of the petition should be paid;

(vii) details of the extent of funding required to enable the company to continue trading during the period of protection, including the sources of funding; and

(viii) any other relevant matters.

25. During the hearing of the petition the independent expert may be questioned on oath and cross examined on aspects of the work they carried out and the reasoning leading to the formation of the opinion that the company has a reasonable prospect of survival as a going concern.

26. There may be cases where the independent expert's report is not available at the time of presenting the petition. In such cases, the court must be satisfied that the reasons for this are due to exceptional circumstances outside the control of the petitioner and could not have been reasonably anticipated by the petitioner.

27. The court may make an order placing the company under the protection of the court for such period as the court thinks appropriate to allow for the submission of the independent expert's report. If the deadline is not met, the company will cease to be under the court's protection.

28. The independent expert is required to supply a copy of their report to the company concerned or any interested party where a written application has been received by the independent expert. Certain parts of the report may be redacted with court permission.

Independent Expert's Report – Other Considerations

29. International Standard on Assurance Engagements (ISAE) 3000 (Revised) 'Assurance Engagements Other than Audits or Reviews of Historical Financial' provides a framework for assurance engagements,

other than audits of historical financial information and is effective for assurance reports dated on or after 15 December 2015.

30. The preparation of the independent expert's report constitutes an assurance engagement as defined under ISAE 3000. As such, it is encouraged to consider the requirements of the standard. ISAE 3000 is available at www.IFAC.org/IAASB.

Practical Considerations

31. Given the significance of the independent expert's report, together with the obligatory and evidential nature of the report as supporting evidence to the petition for appointment of an examiner, the expert should be conscious of practical matters, which may preclude them from accepting the assignment or being able to form the opinion that the company and the whole or any part of its undertaking would have a reasonable prospect of survival as a going concern.

32. Examples of circumstances that could constrain the expert, include:

   (i)   time constraints, including where a petition is made within 3 days of a receiver's appointment;

   (ii) lack of information and/or satisfactory evidence to support the directors' "belief" that appointment of an examiner would save some or all of the company's business; and

   (iii) The cumulative impact of significant caveats and/or uncertainties referred to within the report where that report expresses the opinion the appointment of an examiner would be more advantageous than liquidation.

The Examiner

Notification of Appointment

33. The examiner must arrange for the publication of their appointment as examiner to the company in *Iris Oifigúil* within 21 days, and two daily newspapers circulating in the district of the registered office of the company within 3 days, of the date of the appointment.

34. The examiner must deliver a copy of the order appointing them as examiner to the Registrar of Companies within 3 days of the date of appointment.

Overview of the Role of the Examiner

35. The examiner must act independently of the company, its Board of Directors, shareholders, creditors, or prospective investors.

36. The company's directors remain responsible for its operations following the examiner's appointment. Accordingly, if contacted directly by the company's creditors, the examiner should inform the creditor that ongoing trade is between the creditor and the company, which is under the control of the directors.

37. The role of the examiner is to oversee the formulation, acceptance and confirmation of proposals for a compromise or scheme of arrangement to facilitate the survival of the company. The role can vary during the assignment, occasionally being analogous to that of a chairman overseeing the development of proposals, at other times to that of an investment banker seeking new investors for the company, and sometimes to that of an executive director negotiating the proposals. Whilst other parties, including professional advisors, will frequently participate in the process, the examiner retains the statutory responsibility for the formulation and recommendation of the scheme proposals.

38. Professional judgment is exercised to ensure that all stakeholders in the process are dealt with in a manner, which takes account of the commercial and legal issues arising in the development of the compromise or scheme of arrangement. This assists the examiner to form the opinion that they have achieved the best possible outcome for all stakeholders in the process.

39. If the examination is to come to a successful conclusion, the examiner must be able to recommend the proposed compromise or scheme of arrangement to each class of creditor and to the court.

40. When chairing the meetings of each class of creditor, the examiner needs to explain to each class of creditor why the proposed compromise or scheme of arrangement offers a better outcome to that class than a liquidation.

41. The examiner is required to prepare and present a report to the court, which includes proposals for a compromise or scheme of arrangement. The court may: confirm, confirm subject to modifications or refuse to confirm the proposals for the compromise or arrangement.

42. Where the examiner is not able to enter into an agreement with interested parties or formulate proposals for a compromise or scheme of arrangement, the examiner should without delay apply to court for direction. The court may give directions or make an order as it deems fit, including, an order for the winding up of the company.

Report of the Examiner

43. The examiner is required to provide an examiner's report, including proposals for a compromise or scheme of arrangement within

35 days of the date of their appointment as examiner or a longer period as the court may see fit.

44. The examiners' report must include:

- the proposals placed before the required meetings;
- any modification of those proposals adopted at any of those meetings;
- the outcome of each of the required meetings;
- the recommendation of the committee of creditors, if any;
- a statement of the assets and liabilities (including contingent and prospective liabilities) of the company as at the date of the report;
- a list of the creditors of the company;
- a list of officers of the company;
- the examiner's recommendations; and
- any other matters the examiner deems appropriate or the court directs.

45. It is expected that an examiner's report will include his recommendation that the confirmation of the proposals will facilitate the survival of the company, and the whole or any part of its undertaking as a going concern. Such a recommendation will typically necessitate meaningful commentary regarding the viability of the business.

46. The examiner must supply a copy of the report to the company, the Office of the Director of Corporate Enforcement (ODCE) and to any interested party on written application.

Examination Process for Small Companies

47. The Act allows an examination process application to be made by an originating Notice of Motion to the Circuit Court as opposed to the High Court, where the company, in respect of its latest financial year-end prior to the date of presentation of the application, meets the definition of a small company under the Act.

48. If the latest financial year of the company ended within three months of the date of the application, then the previous financial year-end shall be used, once that financial year-end is within fifteen months of the date of the application.

49. In the case of *Rathmond Ireland Limited*, where the High Court found that the petitioning company was a small company for the purpose of the Act, the judge appointed the examiner and remitted the case to the Circuit Court for all further hearings. The court indicated that in the case of a small company, as defined in the Act, it was inappropriate to petition in the High Court.

Powers and Duties of Directors

50. The powers and duties of directors are generally unchanged following the appointment of an examiner to the company. The obligation to maintain the company's statutory records, including its accounting records remains with the directors.
51. The Examiner has power to convene, set the agenda, attend and preside at meetings of directors, and may apply to the court for an order conferring on him the powers of directors. In exceptional cases, he may apply to exercise the powers of a liquidator in relation to the company.
52. Section 526 of the Act states "It shall be the duty of the officers and agents of a company to which an examiner has been appointed to:
    (a) produce to the examiner all books and documents of, or relating to, any such company which are in their custody or power,
    (b) attend before the examiner when required by the examiner so to do, and
    (c) otherwise give to the examiner all assistance in connection with the examiner's functions which they are reasonably able to give."

Updated

53. This Statement was updated on 1 January 2018.

Appendix C.
The Examinership Timeline

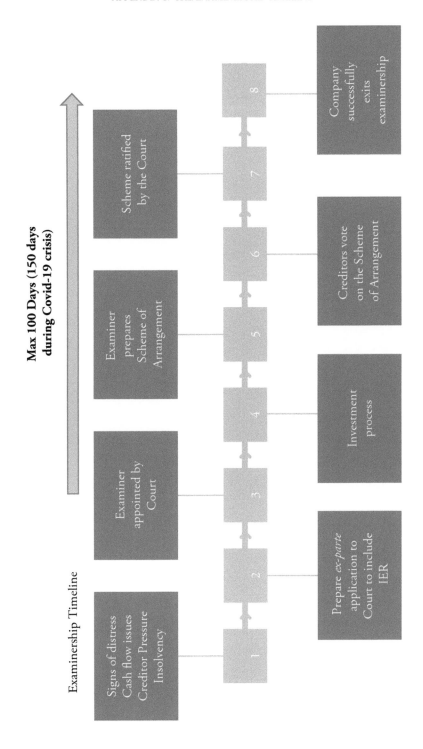

Index

independent experts' reports (IERs)
  contents of
    cash-flow projections, 50, 77,
      104, 111
    company background, 73
    company history, 73
    financial history, 73–4
    future prospects of company, 75
    identification of onerous
      leases, x156
    management team details, 75–6
    pre-petition liabilities payment
      recommendations, 80–81, 96,
      114, 123
    reasonable prospect of survival
      opinion, 21, 49–50, 71–2, 76
    sources of financial difficulties, 74
    statement of affairs, 72, 78–80
    taxation liabilities, 74–5
    trading projections, 51, 75
  cost of, 72, 165
  examiner's review of assertions
    in, 104
  introduction of, 21, 67
  overview, 71–2
  parties qualifying as independent
    experts, 69
  presentation in petition
    paperwork, 85, 94
information memorandums (IMs),
  131–2
insolvency
  balance sheet test, 49, 74
  cash-flow test, 49, 74
  causes of, 3, 34, 59
  EU Directive on restructuring, 175–8
  numbers of cases, 7, 176
  procedures for dealing with see
    examinership; liquidation;
    receivership
  as requirement for entering examin-
    ership, 49, 73–4
  as result of a once-off event, 58
insolvency clauses, 35
insolvency fatigue, 52
Insolvency Service of Cyprus, 68

Institute of Certified Public Accountants of Cyprus (ICPAC), 68
insurance claims, 61
insurance premiums, 80, 96, 114, 123
intangible assets, 35–6, 52, 73, 169
integrity, 53, 62
intellectual property, 35, 52, 83, 116, 169
interim examiners, 23–4, 67, 84, 85–6,
  93, 125, 170
International Monetary Fund (IMF), 4, 176
investment agreements, 119, 136
investment process
  due diligence, 132, 133
  escrow agreements, 119, 136, 159
  exclusivity period, 133–4
  expressions of interest, 131
  funding sources
    existing directors or sharehold-
      ers, 38–9, 125, 129–30
    new investment, 5, 38–9, 61, 131–4
    re-financing, 5, 61, 120–21, 130
    sale of non-core assets, 61, 135–6
    surplus cash flows, 61, 134–5
  information memorandums, 131–2
  investment agreements, 119, 136
  investment proposal selection, 132–3
  non-disclosure agreements, 131
  providing transparency and cer-
    tainty for investors, 38–9
investment proposals, 132–3
invoice discounting, 87, 107–8, 112–13,
  122, 130
Iris Oifigiúil, 106

Jack & Jones, 123
J.D. Brian Limited, 25
job protection, 6–7, 20, 31, 34–5, 51,
  60–61, 120, 175
Joe.ie *see* Maximum Media Networks
  Limited
joint examiners, 69–70
joint liquidators, 69–70
joint receivers, 69–70
JP McKenna & Sons Limited, 167
JP Transpeed Express Portlaoise
  Limited, 31